HOW TO MARRY A MULTI-MILLIONAIRE

THE ULTIMATE GUIDE TO HIGH NET WORTH DATING

by Ted Morgan and Serena Worth

SPECIALIST PRESS INTERNATIONAL

New York

For further information, contact:

SPECIALIST PRESS INTERNATIONAL

99 Spring Street, 3rd Floor
New York, NY 10012
Tel: (212) 431-5011
Fax: (212) 431-8646
E-mail: *publicity@spibooks.com*
Visit us at *www.spibooks.com*

10 9 8 7 6 5 4 3 2 1
First Edition

Library of Congress Cataloging-in-Publication Data available.
ISBN: 1-56171-884-x

DEDICATION

To: Kate Bohner, Sydney Biddle Barrows, Carah Von Funk,
Dyan Machan, Diana Butler, Anne Templeton, C.B., B.E.E.,
A.W.R.F., R.F., E.G.S. and
women of ambition everywhere.

CONTENTS

INTRODUCTION

IT'S NOT ABOUT THE MONEY– SUCCESSFUL MEN ARE JUST SEXIER

Most women don't list wealth or appearance as the most important characteristic in a mate. The most common qualities cited by women in a desirable man are confidence, charm, humor, intelligence, and aggressiveness. We all prefer a man who knows who he is and loves what he does.

Of course, these are primary characteristics possessed by most wealthy and successful men. In the business world you simply don't make it unless you are smart, confident and aggressive and know what you want. Even if they don't have it naturally, successful men develop humor and charm as tools from their experience in dealing with others. Most very high net worth men are quite charming, although they may sometimes appear brash and forceful to the point of rudeness or even bad taste. They are who they are and they want you to know it. This is a very attractive quality.

Super-successful men are not generally shy, uncertain, tentative or insecure about what they want (although they may be vain and insecure in other ways). The nice thing about super-successful men is they won't waste your time if they don't want you. If they make an effort to be with you it's because they want to be with you.

And what woman doesn't want a man who wants her?

"It's not really about the money," says Kelley, a lithe tanned brunette with deep sea green eyes. "I love self-made men because there's tremendous security in knowing that whatever happens, they have what it takes to bounce right back. And there's something else. When a self made man flies you to Paris for the weekend in his private jet, you know he's doing it because he wants to be with you. Because there's a lot of other things he could be doing with his time."

It isn't just the cash that makes these men sexy. But the cash is a very nice side benefit.

Let's be practical. We all want a nice home, a good car, great clothes, vacations at a fashionable resort and the means to entertain our friends and raise our children in reasonable comfort and style. We want to put our children through a good college and we want decent jewelry to wear when we go out.

Does this make us all Gold Diggers?

No way!

Is this too much to ask?

Of course not.

Now go back and add up the cost of the basic items we just mentioned. Then figure out the income you would need to cover the after-tax cost of those items and to put away a nest egg for your retirement. Now let's assume you live in New York City, Los Angeles or another expensive urban center.

Finished calculating?

For these basic needs you will require pretax income of at least $500,000 annually.

Now (if you are lucky enough to have a job) look at your pay stub for last month and multiply the income shown by 12.

Surprise!

It's not enough to cover even these basic needs. If you are like most working women, you will need at least 10 to 20 times what you are now earning to raise a family in reasonable comfort. And you may have a job where you will not be able to advance if you pause to have even one child, much less two or three.

Your dream life is already running a big deficit and you haven't even started yet!

Who is going to make up the difference?

Your future husband, that's who.

But where are you going to find a man who wants to marry you who makes a half million dollars a year? You aren't even meeting guys like that. How are you going to get one of these guys—that you aren't even meeting—to marry you?

It gets worse.

You don't even want a guy who makes $500,000 a year.

Why not?

Because $500,000 is not nearly enough money!

What about that second house in the Hamptons or Palm Beach? They can easily run you another $2 million to $35 million each or more. Not to mention a car for you, a live-in nanny, the maids in the city and the country, your spa treatments and yoga classes, your lunches at The Four Seasons and additional plastic surgery as you get into your 40s. And what about your jet? I mean who wants to fly commercial anyway?

But there's more. What about that Bulgari watch you've had your eye on? Not to mention the $85,000 annual membership fee for the Southampton Bath and Tennis Club and $100,000 for the campaign to get in. And then there's another $6,000 a month in charity benefits just so you have something to do in the evenings. And you don't want to have to worry about financial reversals, stock market declines and all those beastly lay-offs on Wall Street.

No. Your husband must have a cushion. Your husband must have a minimum net worth of at least $10 million with current annual income in excess of one million dollars.

Now we are beginning to talk some sense.

"We want love, but we expect money," we were told by a former Ms. Michigan and the winner of 25 other beauty pageants. "Most of my New York girlfriends won't date anyone who makes less than one million dollars a year." But this beauty, who is independently wealthy, says she can afford "to go down to $300,000."

There are approximately 100,000 men in the United States with a net worth of over $10 million dollars and an annual income in excess of $1 million. Over half of them live in Manhattan, Los Angeles, Palm Beach and Aspen. There are about 160 million women living in America today.

Guess what? Those millions of women all want the same thing you do. This priceless book will show you how to beat the odds and outsmart all 159.9 million of them while you land yourself a high net worth husband.

Here's how to get started:

(1) Buy this book immediately!

(2) Get down to your fighting weight using the Gold Digger's Diet™ explained in this book.

(3) Consult a top plastic surgeon to correct any obvious flaws and to enhance your appearance.

(4) Move to Manhattan.

(5) Get on the social scene, identify your knight in shining armor, pull him off his high horse.

Grab Your Knight in Shining Armor by the *Cojones*!

Your husband-to-be is not going to descend from heaven on a white steed clad in shining armor. He is not going to come charging through your life and scoop you onto his horse and carry you away to the big house on the beach of your dreams. He is not going to call you while you sit at home waiting for the phone to ring.

You are going to have to get out there and find your sexy mogul and pull him off his horse by the balls! Otherwise he will continue on his way seeking other women until he meets his match. Who is his match? The girl who can knock his horse unconscious with a good right hook while standing upright in her Manolo Blahniks and holding a champagne glass in her left hand.

We don't care who you are or where you live. As long as you are under 35-years-old and don't have a face like a bashed crab you can marry a high net worth man following the steps listed in this book. And if you do have a face like a bashed crab, get it fixed and then follow the steps in this book. If you are over 35 years of age don't despair. You can always work the senior circuit which in many ways can be more lucrative than regular league play.

If you want to be poor, by all means sit at home waiting for your phone to ring. If you want a great life with the big lifestyle that comes with it, buy this book now and get out there and fight for it!

PART ONE

High Net Worth Mating

CHAPTER ONE

THE HONORABLE GOLD DIGGER

Taking Care of Number One

There is nothing wrong with true love. If you can find it. The problem is most people never do. And women who sit around passively waiting for their true love to walk into their life and find them are bound to be disappointed. The only thing that will find them is old age.

While we should never give up the hope of finding true love, in the meantime looking out for number one is the most effective strategy for individual survival. There really is no meaningful alternative to a strategy of self-interest.

A woman exists primarily to fulfill her own needs and desires. Her ultimate concern must be herself and her well being. Securing her financial security and comfort with an exciting and successful high net worth man is a key goal for every intelligent, aggressive woman.

The best way to secure your future for yourself and your children is to marry a man who is rich enough and capable enough to survive comfortably through any foreseeable financial reversal.

Women need to secure their financial future while they are still of childbearing age so they can raise a family in comfort. Even high-powered Wall Street careers will rarely allow a woman time to amass enough wealth to retire and raise a family in style and comfort.

If you graduate from business school between 23-25 years of age, it will take you at least 10 years to achieve the rank of Managing Director at a Wall Street investment bank. Even if you stay there working 16 hour days and claw your way to the top, you will just be reaching your peak earning power as your fertility begins to decline precipitously. This is the time when many professional women panic and start desperately trying to seek a husband. At this point you are negotiating from a position of weakness. Your dates can see the desperation in your eyes. And the anxiety about missing the chance to have children will adversely affect and may even overwhelm your emotional well-being and can damage your high-powered career.

But if you start planning in your 20s and focus on marrying a rich man with the same dedication you would devote to a Wall Street career, you are much more likely to be rewarded with success and a great lifestyle.

Do you really want to end up as a haggard, overworked, over-wrought, childless and single middle-aged woman? Or do you want to get out there and fight for a successful, intelligent and dynamic high net worth man now, while you can still get one.

The choice is yours.

A Time-Honored Profession

Marrying wealth is a time-honored profession. It is best distinguished from the World's oldest profession by one important fact. It is older.

And, of course, wives and mothers are not usually paid by the hour.

It doesn't matter where you live. It doesn't matter where you are now. It does not matter what you do for a living. Even if you are stuck on a dirt farm in Arkansas or lying in rags on a bearskin rug in a cave in Siberia, if you are an attractive woman, you can land a wealthy husband by getting on the next plane to New York City. You don't even need to speak much English. All you need is a shower, a manicure, pedicure, high heels and a great outfit. Then get on the high net worth dating circuit. Charge your tickets to the important charity benefits listed later in this book and get out there and date. The world is about to become your playground.

You Add Value

As an ambitious woman, you should think of yourself as a value added service provider. You should not seek positions where you are insufficiently compensated for the value you add to your man's life.

An ambitious woman can provide the following diverse array of services to her wealthy companion or significant other. She offers:

(1) Charming companionship
(2) Intense sex
(3) Social graces
(4) Arm and eye candy (yourself and your attractive girlfriends)
(5) Potential wife and mother material for his unborn heirs
(6) A helpmate to organize his social and professional life.
(7) Interior decorator for multiple residences and the Gulf Stream.

Finding a High Net Worth Mate is a Full-Time Job

In fulfilling all of these roles or in seeking a position as a wife or mistress you will have overhead. You will have expenses. Your income must cover all the following expenses and fund a healthy nest egg for your future retirement (in case, despite all of your good efforts, you never do land that high profile husband):

(**1**) Apartment or house
(**2**) Gym and personal trainer
(**3**) Spa treatments
(**4**) Manicure and pedicure
(**5**) High-end hair salon
(**6**) Large wardrobe of sexy clothes for any possible occasion from an outdoor barbecue, to the beach, to the Metropolitan Museum Gala Costume Institute Party, to summer and winter cocktail parties, ski trips, dinners and business conferences.
(**7**) La Perla, Wolford, Eres and Agent Provocateur underwear
(**8**) High-end handbags
(**9**) Shoes, shoes, shoes
(**10**) And last but not least, especially in the later years, plastic surgery.

This adds up to a great deal of cash. You may be tempted to take a full-time job. That could be a mistake. Not having a steady source of income while piling up huge debts will actually incentivize you to be bolder in seizing high net worth dating opportunities.

Besides, you don't have time to work!

Chapter Two

The Tao of Gold Digging

Gold Digging is an art. To learn it well you must understand the basic principles and philosophy of the successful Gold Digger. The following Golden Rules can be used to successfully organize your life.

THE 10 GOLDEN RULES

(1) Life is a business and nature is a free market system.
(2) Your appearance is your most important economic asset.
(3) Marriage can be a very lucrative occupation.
(4) You will get the job if you add value.
(5) Good is what's good for you.
(6) Evil is anything not in your interest.
(7) What he likes about you is not about you.
(8) Morality is an opinion.
(9) Rejection is information.
(10) The best things in life are very expensive.

THE 10 GOLDEN RULES EXPLAINED

Life is a Business and Nature is a Free Market System

You only get gold by giving it. You will only marry a rich man if you can demonstrate the value you add to his life. Don't count on him marrying you for love. It isn't going to happen unless you show him how you can be an asset to him. And since nature is a free market system you can claw your way to the top just as men do in business. You just can't be quite so obvious.

Your Appearance is Your Most Important Economic Asset

Beauty is among the highest accomplishments for a woman. Beauty is a sign of genetic health. That's why men are attracted to beautiful women. Your job is to make yourself look beautiful whenever you go out in public. Beauty creates possibilities. Looking good is an economic asset. Your man wants a beautiful woman on his arm. Your beauty is not about you. It is an asset to him. If he doesn't think you look good on him, he won't marry you.

Marriage Can Be a Very Lucrative Occupation

No matter what career you choose, you cannot possibly earn as much money as you will in the position of high net worth wife. Single women can't make enough to afford big houses in Southampton, Aspen, Palm Beach and New York. Don't kid yourself. The position of a wife to a wealthy man is far and away the best paying job you can have.

You Will Get the Job if You Add Value

Being an asset to him in as many ways as possible is the surest way to increase the net assets line in your financial statement. Give him what he wants and needs and he will give you gold (and diamonds too!).

Good is What's Good for You

You've got to start by redefining your values. You must realize that good and bad can only be judged in relation to a goal. They do not exist in the abstract. Good is when you lure your high net worth fiancé away from your best girlfriend. Good is when you get what you want.

Evil is Anything Not in Your Interest

Evil is when your best girlfriend steals the heart of your fiancé and he ends up marrying her and not you or if he goes back to his ex-girlfriend or wife. Evil is when someone else gets what you want.

What He Likes About You is Not About You

Your prospective husband will like you only to the extent you give him what he wants. He may want you for sex, motherhood, and to be his social director, golf partner, cook and girl Friday. He may want you because he likes to lick your toes. He may like you because you know a lot about decorating or cooking. He may like you because you have good genes or large breasts or a distinguished family name. Whatever the reason, don't forget that these are all qualities that are assets to him.

Morality is an Opinion

Your job is to get your guy, not to speculate on the moral fabric of the universe. It is rare that two people's views of morality will coincide. Don't worry about the morality of marrying for money, worry about your waistline and the size of your ass. That is far more productive.

Rejection is Information

Rejection means you are in the game. If you never want to be rejected you might as well give up now. Rejection is something you learn from. What you learn is what your guy wants. Whether he wants you or doesn't want you the reasons will be his reasons. Rejection just means he didn't perceive you as a significant asset to his life. Sometimes this happens when a man figures out what you are really up to.

The Best Things in Life Are Very Expensive

Private schools, ski vacations, good jewelry, palatial homes and high-end handbags come at a steep price. The only way to afford them (unless you are one of the lucky few who inherited substantial wealth), is to get someone to buy them for you. And believe us when we tell you that, except in very unusual circumstances, he will not be buying you a palatial home unless you are married to him.

THE 10 GOLDEN COMMANDMENTS –
A FRAMEWORK FOR ACTION

Once you understand the 10 Golden Rules you are ready for the 10 Golden Commandments. The 10 Golden Commandments give you the framework for action you need to snare a high net worth husband.

(1) In every relationship, always ask, "What's in it for me?"

(2) Help yourself and let others help themselves.

(3) Know what you want.

(4) Be energetic and persistent in pursuing your man.

(5) Know when to break the rules.

(6) Don't be nice, be charming and sexy.

(7) Be flexible and aware of shifting opportunities.

(8) Don't get angry, get what you want.

(9) Don't be negative.

(10) Understand that what others do is not about you.

THE 10 GOLDEN COMMANDMENTS EXPLAINED

In Every Relationship, Always Ask, "What's in it for me?"

This is the key question in every phase of human interaction. If you don't know what you are getting out of the situation, why are you in it? If you can't answer this question it is often because you are doing something to please another person, not yourself. This will usually end up making you unhappy. Don't do things to please other people, do them to please yourself.

Help Yourself and Let Others Help Themselves

Worry about yourself. If you want to help a person, do so because it provides some benefit to you. Helping others with no benefit to yourself is a symptom of low self-esteem and a recipe for personal failure. Saying of others "she's out for herself" is not a very pointed criticism. After all, who with any sense isn't?

Know What You Want

If you don't know what you want you are never going to get it. Some women don't want to marry a rich man. Some women don't want to be able to buy anything they want. We don't know who these women are but we see them everywhere, working in meaningless office jobs, cleaning up office buildings, working in the supermarket or the post office or just walking around looking aimless and bored. These women don't realize that if you don't know what you want no one else will.

Be Energetic and Persistent in Pursuing Your Man

Life is a process of trying something, bumping up against an obstacle and being repulsed, then trying something different until finally you have a breakthrough and achieve your goal. Since you will constantly run into obstacles, you will be defeated if you lack the energy and persistence to get around them. When you run into an obstacle, instead of getting discouraged, try to see what opportunity the new obstacle presents. You may find that what looked like an obstacle may actually be something that can help you get your guy.

Know When to Break the Rules

Rules are for other people. Don't obey rules for their own sake. They were not made for your benefit. Crashing a big charity benefit or a party you weren't invited to may be against the rules but if you do it you may be able to meet a number of eligible high net worth men. No one will thank you for obeying the rules and staying home to watch TV because you can't afford a benefit ticket or because it is sold out or you weren't invited. On the other hand you should not take extreme risks with long-term adverse consequences. Committing violent crimes of aggression to sabotage your girlfriend's efforts to land the man you want is unlikely to be the most efficient way to achieve your goal. Simply undermine your rivals with malicious gossip. It is not necessary to physically kill them. Deciding whether to break or bend a rule is simply a matter of balancing the relative costs and benefits of the alternative courses of action.

Don't Be Nice, Be Charming and Sexy

Being charming, sexy and flirtatious is an important tool for getting what you want from another person. Being nice is weak because it does not ask for anything. Don't be nice gratuitously, but always be charming. The positive energy you exude can reap enormous benefits by attracting people to you who can help you get what you want.

Be Flexible and Aware of Shifting Opportunities

Circumstances are constantly changing. Your sensitivity and awareness of what is going on around you are your most important tools for getting what you want. By being aware of other people's needs and desires, you can figure out what you can offer them to get them to do what you want. The key to life is being in the moment. If you are distracted, tired, cross or grumpy, you will miss numerous opportunities around you. You are most likely to be in the moment when you are well rested, look good and feel confident. If you are in the zone, you will have a much more positive experience of life. If you are grumpy and negative, you will repel rather than attract people and you will lose out on the possibilities they offer.

Don't Get Angry, Get What You Want

Anger is frustration at your own impotence in the face of a failure to get what you want. It is childish, tantrum-like, and has no place in your repertoire of emotions. If you are successful at getting what you want, you will have no reason to be angry. And if you fail to get what you want, it's usually because you made a mistake or miscalculation or failed to take into account an external circumstance or another person's action. This is a reason to do better next time. It is not a reason to be angry. So don't go psycho! Go shopping instead.

Don't Be Negative

Positive action requests a positive result. Being negative doesn't work because it does not ask for anything positive to happen. Criticism can be great fun but it won't solve the problem. Only positive action solves problems. Being negative repels other people instinctively because they know it is not a successful strategy. And other people won't want to be around you if they perceive you are an unsuccessful person. By being negative, you are waving a sign post that reads "I don't know how to get what I want. All I know how to do is complain."

Understand That What Others Do Is Not About You

Other people do things for their own reasons. They usually don't do them intentionally to help or hurt you. They are just trying to get what they want. You may be in the way or you may not be. The best way to avoid the energy drain and friction that comes from confrontation is to stay out of the way of other people when it does not hurt you to do so. There is no point in having a confrontation over the fact that someone shoved you in the subway. It's simply energy draining and a complete waste of time. The Manolo Blahniks sample sale? That's a situation where you should get aggressive. Grab that last pair of silver stilettos right out of the hands of that pushy publicist ahead of you, sweetie!

CHAPTER THREE

THINGS YOU SHOULD KNOW ABOUT MEN

Men Are Not a Mystery

Many women are constantly puzzled by the behavior of men. These women keep expecting men to act like women and are surprised when they don't.

Men are not like women. They are, if you will, a different kind of machine. But a machine nonetheless. They behave in very predictable ways, more so perhaps than women.

Here are some characteristics of men that may surprise you.

Men do not talk to each other about relationships

In fact, men do not talk to each other at all. That's how they have time to watch sports. Men do not interpret life in terms of relationships. They interpret life in terms of results. They therefore have a much more black and white view of the world than women.

Men do not care about flowers

When a man gives you a beautiful bouquet you may be moved to tears. But he won't care about them at all. He is giving them to you to make you do something he wants you to do or to prevent you from doing something he doesn't want you to do (like dumping him). Most likely the flowers were chosen by his secretary. The only input he had was to say, "Don't go over $65." When you call to tell him how beautiful they are, keep in mind that he probably has no idea what he sent you.

Men do not even like flowers. If they did, they would give them to each other.

Men are visually oriented

Men are initially attracted to you by your physical appearance. (Hence the importance of looking good). A man will almost never ask you out unless he is pleased and excited by your physical appearance.

A man may like you because you have nice feet. He may like you because you have large breasts or he may like you because you have long legs or beautiful eyes and thick pouty lips. It does not matters what he likes about you. He may call you obsessively because he is fantasizing about sucking your toes or having sex with you from behind. This does not mean he cares about you. In fact, you can be sure that he doesn't. You haven't had time for him to bond to you. But you can still reel him in using the things he likes about you even if a continuing exclusive relationship is not initially on his agenda.

Healthy heterosexual men are not naturally monogamous

Men like to fool around. Given the chance they will. This is nothing personal. If they don't cheat on you it's not because they don't want to, it's because they value your relationship more than they do the chance for casual sex, or they may just be lacking opportunities to cheat. All things being equal, however, the majority of men will cheat on you if they have the opportunity.

Men are attracted to women of childbearing years

While you may grow old, your man will continue to be attracted to women of childbearing years. Women can be quite comfortable with a much older man. Men, on the other hand, are genetically biologically programmed to be primarily attracted to women who are under 35-years old. Men are designed to want children and they select mates that are capable of having them. That's why many wealthy men trade in their wives for a younger woman every 10 years or so. This is not because men are evil or selfish. This is simply because they are men. Men want to be with a woman of childbearing years even if they don't want to have children. This is why you must be prepared to fight for a big divorce settlement if he decides to trade you in.

Sex becomes more and more infrequent the more time you spend together. However, his sex drive is by no means diminished.

There is an old joke that there is no sex after marriage. After a year or so of marriage you may find that this joke is on you. Your man will usually grow tired of having sex with you. This is a very bad sign for the future of your relationship, because you can be sure that his sex drive has not diminished. Your man just isn't finding you as the outlet he wants anymore.

A Man likes to please a woman, but he must feel that he can please her

A man will dump a woman he is very attracted to physically if he feels he cannot please her. Men like to please women. But a woman who is constantly and relentlessly demanding will not hold on to her man because he will soon realize that no matter what he does he can never please her. This will make him miserable. More importantly, it will make him dump her. Encourage your man by showing him that he can make you happy. That will make him happy.

Men can be broken

Ask any woman who has been married five years or more. She has found the way to break down her man by getting him into a routine of being with her. Eventually they get used to the idea of being with you. After that he may get used to the idea of not being with other women, although in many cases this is a longer process. The point is you can succeed in breaking him down by subtly working your way into every aspect of his life.

Men can't read your mind and don't want to

Worse than that they don't have a clue what is in it. That's why you must communicate clearly what you expect of him. Communicate in a clear but positive and upbeat way what it is you want him to do. He will want to please you if you show him you care. Being angry with him will just turn him off to you. If you yell at him you can be sure he won't do what you want. Don't expect him to know what you want. The thing you want would probably never occur to him in a thousand years. It's up to you to communicate your needs and desires. If you don't, no one else will.

Men view how you look as a reflection on them

No man wants to be seen with an unattractive or unpresentable woman. Every man wants to be seen with a beautiful woman on his arm. This is the highest status a man can achieve. There is nothing more humiliating for a man than to be seen with an ugly woman. From his perspective your looks are not about you, they are assets to him. If you don't look good enough to make him proud he will drop you. And he may do so after years of marriage. The high net worth man's nagging desire to trade up is an issue you will be facing throughout your tenure as a high net worth wife. Keep in mind that because he is rich he will always be able to replace you if he wants to. Protect yourself financially in case disaster strikes. It can arrive with startling swiftness.

Life is a Business; Marrying a High Net Worth Man is a Job

Life is a business and human beings are traders by nature. Your man will only care about you if he perceives that you are adding value to his life. You add value by being presentable to his friends, colleagues, family and strangers, by being an asset in his life and by giving him what he wants in bed. Unless you are providing value you can be sure he won't marry you. No employer will hire a person who can't do the job. Your knight in the shining silver jet will certainly not marry you unless he perceives you as someone who can provide continuing value. Being his wife is a very lucrative opportunity which can provide lifetime security and benefits for you and your future children. In exchange you will be expected to supervise and decorate multiple households, arrange social events, bear his children, be available for sex (whenever and however he wants it), make sure his life runs smoothly and look damn good doing it.

It won't be easy but it will be well worth it!

CHAPTER FOUR

THE MOGUL PERSONALITY

If you are going to dig for real gold, you had better understand what you are getting into. While every mogul is different, with many unique positive and negative characteristics, the super-successful man will usually have the following qualities:

(1) *He will be confident.*

One of the most attractive qualities of the super-successful man is his highly developed sense of self-confidence. He knows who he is and he knows what he wants. If he wants you he means it.

(2) *He will be very intelligent.*

The super-successful man has a piercing intelligence that often gives him the ability to unravel extremely complex and difficult circumstances and see through to the most probable end result and how it will affect him. Such men often have a unique eye-opening perspective on the world because they see things so differently from the mass of ordinary people.

One mogul we know who had just bought a gay newspaper in a

major city to help with his liberal wife's election campaign was being lambasted in the press by gay activists for buying the newspaper in what they viewed as a Wall Street takeover of an important gay media outlet. When we asked this mogul how he felt about the thrashing he was getting from the press his response was certainly counter-intuitive:

"We think it's great," he said. "It's free publicity for the paper which will make mainstream advertisers comfortable that they can advertise with us without being identified with the radical gay element. This will increase our revenue between 20 and 30%." Of course he was right.

(3) He will be a risk taker.

You may find your mogul repeatedly gambling his existing assets to build something bigger. Your stomach may be permanently experiencing that sinking feeling from the incredible risks he is willing to take. But don't worry. Even when they fail, these guys can usually pick themselves up and get back on their feet in very short order. Read *Trump: The Art of the Comeback*, by co-authors Kate Bohner and Donald J. Trump, for a good example of how a mogul made it back from the precipice.

(4) He has a low level of fear.

While he may not be completely fearless, he will be unafraid to be himself and will be much less afraid of external circumstances than the ordinary person.

(5) He will be extremely energetic.

He may not need much sleep. He will have the energy to run you ragged.

(6) He will be charming.

Even when a successful man lacks social skills he will have charm. If he is charmless he is unlikely to stay successful.

(7) He will be aware of the surrounding circumstances and people to the extent that they affect him.

He knows how others perceive him and he will have a sense (perhaps a somewhat exaggerated sense) of his own power.

(8) He will be determined and persistent, even ruthless in getting what he wants.

He may perceive obstacles as opportunities and if he really wants something he will not take "No" for an answer.

(9) *He will be optimistic and positive in dealing with others.*

He will be confident about his ability to get what he wants. That's how he became so successful in the first place.

(10) *He will be extraordinarily, mind-bogglingly selfish.*

The super-successful man always asks what is in it for him. His ultimate concern is himself. It will be a challenge to make him care about you.

(11) *He will be controlling, demanding and impatient.*

The super-successful are used to getting their own way. Quickly. And watch out for detectives. You may find that he is controlling to the point of having you followed or kept under surveillance.

(12) *He may be one or more of the following*:
  (i) Narcissistic;
  (ii) Charismatic;
  (iii) Secretive;
  (iv) Stingy;
  (v) Angry and irritable in private;
  (vi) Difficult to bond with;
  (vii) An insomniac;
  (viii) Of large girth or appetites;
  (ix) Vengeful; or
  (x) A liar.

(13) *He will understand that life is a business.*

He will want to know what value you can add to his life.

Mogul personalities are often very difficult to live with if you fight with them for control. They may clash with a strong independent woman. Mogul personalities like to control the people around them. Sometimes they control people by taking care of them. In effect they want to own you. There is no point in fighting with him over this. You are not going to win. With the mogul personality, demonstrating your financial independence may make him uncomfortable. He will like to pay for you and give you gifts. This is something you should be able to learn to accept.

The Trump Dump

It was pitch-black in the auditorium. Donald Trump was bellowing through the public address system: "We had the best year ever!" The employees cheered. It was the holidays. The Plaza Hotel in New York City. The Trump Organization Christmas party. December 23, 1998.

Kate Bohner had spent the past 12 months writing *Trump: The Art of the Comeback.* Like many business magazine journalists, she had jumped at the chance to write what had to become a bestseller. So here she was, six months hence – after *Trump: The Art of the Comeback* had indeed become a bestseller, number 3 on *The New York Times* list and number 1 for *The Wall Street Journal.*

"Now I want to talk about my book ..." cooed The Donald into the microphone. "Kateso, you here?" His ruddy, bloated face floats above the microphone. He scanned the room. "Kateso!" he barked.

Kate raised her hand from the back of the ballroom.

"I'm the only person who has a ghost writer whose picture is on the back of the book," the Donald continued. The crowd chuckled. "But hey, she's kind of great looking." The room bursts into applause.

Later that evening, as the bad 12-piece band blared, Kate Bohner approached the Donald. She had something very important to go over with him. It was about the book.

The deal was this. She got paid 60K for the manuscript – in three installments.

"Kateso," The Donald had told her back in May. "If the book goes above number five on *The New York Times Bestseller List* ... I'll bonus you 100 grand."

The book was at Number 3. Kate was at the Christmas party to collect her promised bonus.

A bit later, Kate approached The Donald. He was perched by the shrimp platter. "Hey Donald, what about my 100 grand?"

"Kateso," he turned and narrowed his eyes. "Sue me," he declared coldly.

Kate was stunned.

But why was she shocked?

Over the past year, in the course of writing the book, Kate told us she had watched The Donald offer 10 cents on the dollar to settle a bill he owed to a contractor with four kids who had just lost a big job. She had seen him fire that contractor's brother, a steamfitter, on Christmas Day.

The Citibank loan officer who had turned him down for a revolving credit facility in 1995, when he nearly went personally bankrupt? Kate observed The Donald spending hours ensuring that her son would have difficulties getting a commercial lease in New York City.

Why had Kate thought she would be treated any differently?

The truth is it was nothing personal. Trump was just being The Donald. To him it was just business. Kate, unfortunately, hadn't gotten the bonus promise in writing. In Bohner's view, The Donald stiffed her just because he could.

Trump, like every truly successful person, is totally focused on his own needs and desires. His real expertise is taking care of himself. People like Trump seem aggressively selfish...because they are. And it's not necessarily a bad thing.

Study your target carefully. If he has a classic mogul personality, you will be able to fit very nicely into his life on his terms in the classic manner. He pays the bills and you lobby quietly for the things you really want. Whatever power you have will have to be exerted from within the context of your relationship through cajoling and persuasion.

In a sense, the classic mogul personality fits perfectly with the classic gold digger. Both operate on the principal of taking care of number one. He gets control and you get the Blackglama mink coat. That's why so many wealthy men end up with Gold Diggers. In the end, they are made for each other.

PART TWO

Creating a High Net Worth Appearance

(The Gold Digger's Guide to Beauty,
Exercise, Dieting, Makeup and Fashion)

CHAPTER FIVE

BEING PRESENTABLE

When you are tracking big game on the High Net Worth Dating Circuit, you must pay attention to your quarry's surroundings. Understanding his social environment is as important as understanding him. You are not just seducing a single male, you must seduce his friends, parents, business colleagues and children, if any. All of these people have the ability to obstruct your path to the altar. If they don't like you, they may try to poison your relationship with your intended.

Getting the important people to like you, or at least be neutral toward you, requires effort, awareness and attention to detail. You will have to do things that these people perceive as being in their interest.

There are two basic aspects to making your intended happy with your relations with his family, friends and colleagues. The first is being presentable. The second is being an asset.

If you are not presentable, you will never get anywhere with your man. While he may adore sucking your toes, making love to you for hours on end or staying in bed with you for days at a time, if you are not presentable, he will never consider marrying you.

Looking the Part

Being presentable means understanding how he and his friends and family imagine his ideal mate. You must be warm and wholesome when you meet his parents or children. You must project the appearance of a responsible and caring person, not of a sexpot who can barely stand up in her high heels.

Here are some qualities you should display with his friends and family:

(1) **BE GRACIOUS AND ATTENTIVE.**

Talk to everyone. Don't play favorites. If you are both at a party at his house, make sure the guests are comfortable, have been properly introduced and have a drink in their hand. Many rich men are utterly lacking in social skills and are dependent on their girlfriend to keep things moving smoothly at parties. If you do this well, he may begin to become socially dependent on you. He will have a better time when he goes out with you because he sees that you make an effort to attract and please other people. He will know that you know how to handle his family and friends in a positive way. If you are not normally gracious and attentive, take an acting class and pretend to be gracious and attentive.

(2) **YOUR DRESS AND MAKEUP SHOULD CONVEY ELEGANCE AND SIMPLICITY.**

No fake nails or wild nail patterns. No excessive makeup. No wild fishnets at business or family gatherings or on visits with his five-year-old. Convey a positive, wholesome appearance for these important persons in his life.

(3) **ACCENTS.**

There are only two universally acceptable accents. None and British. A heavy New Jersey, Queens, Brooklyn, Midwestern or Boston accent will mark you as an undesirable for life. If you have such an accent, or if you have a harsh, high-pitched or squeaky voice, hire a voice coach and start changing it. There is no point in circulating socially until you have gotten rid of your undesirable accent. High net worth men don't even want a hooker with a Brooklyn accent, much less a wife.

Southern accents can be charming and sexy. Some men are attracted to Southern accents. As long as you sound educated and sophisticated you can keep your Southern accent.

Foreign accents are generally okay and can be a plus. British, French, Italian and Scandinavian or Dutch accents can be very sexy for the high net worth American. U.K. regional or lower class accents such as Jordy, Cockney, Irish or Scottish are not acceptable and should be purged. Unless your last name is Fanjul, heavy Spanish accents are generally not acceptable, even if you are Spanish.

(4) FAT IS NOT PRESENTABLE.

There is only one body type the high net worth man really wants: Tall and thin, or failing that, medium tall and thin. Anything else and you are starting with a significant handicap. We don't care how tall you are. If you weigh more than 150 pounds you are not eligible for major league play.

High net worth men do not date or marry fat women. And if they marry a woman who becomes fat they will usually divorce her. The reasons for this are simple. Men do not like being shamed in front of other men. Being with a fat woman means that all you can get is a genetically undesirable fat person. To be seen with a fat woman is the ultimate humiliation for a man. It's like driving a beat-up car. A normal guy won't go near you if you are fat. While some men are fat fetishists, these men are rarely desirable high net worth targets.

Stay home until you are thin. And when you get thin, never admit you were once fat. He does not want to hear how proud you are of your weight loss accomplishments. He will be thinking only one thing: "She was fat once, she can be fat again!"

(5) HAIR IS ONLY FOR YOUR HEAD.

The only hair on your body should be on the top of your head. In particular, there should be no mustache, no underarm hair, no nipple hair and no hair on your legs. Your pubis should be completely shaved or have a thin, trim line leading down to your vagina. Dark hair on the arms can be just as unattractive as on your legs. Men like you smooth and soft. Men don't like hairy women. They want a Brazilian.

Shave it, wax it, laser it. But whatever you do, get rid of it!

(6) TEETH.

Teeth should be clean, white and bright with a fresh pink tongue. If you have grey or yellow teeth you will have to have them fixed or go get veneers. No one wants to kiss a woman with yellow teeth. Cosmetic dentistry can be the difference between being in the game or out of it.

(7) HANDS AND TOES.

Men do not like to see cracked, chipped or half-painted fingers or toes. If you want a man to think you don't care enough about yourself and him to have a manicure and pedicure, by all means stay home and concentrate on your career. Because you are never going to get married.

Use one solid color. He does not want to see a kaleidoscope when he looks at your feet. And please no blue toenails! If your nails are bitten, half painted or painted in tacky colors it tells a man you don't care what the world thinks of him or you. Don't go on a date unless your nails are flawless.

(8) HIRE AN IMAGE CONSULTANT.

Held back by poor table manners, lousy taste, weak conversational skills, a grating accent, limited education or bad hair? No problem. Hire an image consultant to polish your table manners and dining gestures and to help you achieve a complete professional image which enhances your best attributes while masking your flaws. The folks at Essential Image in New York City will even provide education on "fine food, drinks and wines" and help you "restructure and build . . . a well rounded wardrobe." And yes they can recommend a speech therapist, dietician, cosmetic surgeon and even an orthodontist or dance instructor. By the time they get through with you, you will look in the mirror and think you are seeing a young Brooke Astor!

CHAPTER SIX

THE GOLD DIGGER'S GUIDE TO BEAUTY, MAKEUP AND FASHION

"Sweetie, leave it to the professionals."
–Candace Bushnell

Natural Beauty

"I like to keep my natural oils," says author Candace Bushnell, explaining why she doesn't believe in excessive bathing or shampooing.

Candace Bushnell is not big on over-bathing. For those of you who share her "less is more" approach to personal hygiene, Lorraine Massey's Devachan hair salon in Manhattan's SoHo puts out a line of minimalist products called "No-Poo" and "Low-Poo" hair care products. No-Poo has no detergent and is effectively a rinse. Devachan insists it is better for your hair to minimize detergent in shampoo.

But Candace also has a good philosophy about beauty. "Sweetie, leave it to the professionals," she used to tell then girlfriend, Kate Bohner explaining why she had her hair washed and blown out twice a week at an upper East Side salon.

Hair is key. And the color you want is white blonde. Make sure to do your eyebrows and arms as well and have your color done regularly. No one wants to see your tell-tale black roots. Any trace of grey should be removed immediately. Grey implies you are not of childbearing years. This is certainly not a plus in the business of high net woth dating.

Jewelry

New York is among the few places where you might regularly see receptionists and flight attendants who make about $30,000 or less per year wearing a $25,000 watch. Did they save up to buy it? Certainly not. They went on a few high net worth dates and got the trophy watch as a present.

Your jewelry is important. "It says who you are and where you belong socially," says New York socialite Diana Butler. "There are five pieces of jewelry every New York woman should have. The pearl double choker necklace–they start at $5,000–the diamond stud earrings–up to three-carats per ear–the great Cartier watch and, if she is lucky, a big Tiffany engagement ring (three-carats minimum) and the platinum wedding ring."

Diana (whose friends call her "Di") continued, "Men will sometimes try to pass off a gft of the Cartier Tank stainless steel version as the White Gold Tank." (The stainless version only costs around $2,500. The White Gold Tank is, however, $13,900. The White Gold Tank with diamonds can run from $30,000 to $35,000, depending on the jewels).

"My two best girlfriends each have the White Gold Tank with diamonds," says Di. "A watch like that makes you feel good, even if you don't like yourself."

To Tan or Not to Tan

You have two basic choices–go lily white or go tan. The latent dangers of the tanning machine have deterred many women from looking their best. But the new spray on tans eliminate this problem and give your skin that sexy golden glow that draws men like flies. On balance we favor the spray on tan or even the fake bake from a tanning machine to the lily white look. We've found that in general men prefer a golden sheen to porcelain white skin. It's just sexier.

Sample Sales

Sample sales are a girl's best friend. These special events are one of the great benefits of living in Manhattan. You can buy clothes at rock bottom prices, sometimes at as little as 10% of retail and it is not unusual to find great clothes and accessories at 50% off the wholesale price (or 70%-80% off the retail price).

Finding most sample sales is easy. Some of the best and most accessible are held at the Parsons School of Design on 40th Street and Seventh Avenue. Just walk up the stairs to the second floor. Parsons holds sales for such top designers as Calvin Klein, Gianfranco Ferré, Joseph Abboud, Loro Piana, Malo, Salvatore Ferragamo (you may occassionally witness a shoe riot at these events!), Donna Karan, Bulgari, Mont Blanc, Tourneau and many, many more. Just walk in and sign up for the mailing list and you will soon be invited to all these sales. The same mailing list will get you invited to various other sales held at 20 West 57th Street, including Elie Tahari, and various accessory labels. Getting invited to the Chanel and Hermès sales on the other hand is an invitation-only affair that requires that you know someone. However, anyone who is hooked-up with the fashion or media crowd should be able to work you in.

Some sample sales are tricky and start a day earlier than the invitation indicates. The first day is reserved for favorite customers. But the security is often very lax. If you know about the sale you can generally walk in.

Beware of touts holding up signs for sample sales on the street. These are rarely worth a visit. The real sales don't advertise, they simply send a private invitation.

Don't turn your nose up at sample sales. The stuff you find there is often very high-end. It hasn't sold precisely because it is so expensive that regular people simply cannot afford it. But at the sample sale price you can have it for yourself. And you never need set foot in a crowded department store or boutique.

There is a newsletter devoted entirely to sample sales called the S&B Report. Save money by subscribing to it with a friend or find a friend who already gets it and you will be clued into a whole world of discount high-fashion. Or check in at the *Daily Candy* (www.dailycandy.com) for similar information. In New York you can do virtually all your shopping at sample sales until you land your high net worth man.

Then you can convert to full price shopping. On his credit card, of course!

CHAPTER SEVEN

THE GOLD DIGGER'S GUIDE TO EXERCISE

Exercise, Exercise, Exercise!

Any dietician will tell you that exercise is a key part of any diet. This is especially true for the Gold Digger's Diet™.

Gold Diggers have a simple rule for determining if they are exercising enough: If you are still getting your period, you may not be exercising enough.

What kind of exercise should I do?

The answer is: aerobic, aerobic, aerobic.

The first and best exercise is running. Run three to five miles or until you drop, whichever comes first. Then pick yourself off the ground and take a cardio kick or step class. Finish up with an hour-and-a-half of spinning. Then eat close to nothing all day.

What we do when we exercise is we sweat, sweat, sweat. This gets the toxins out and burns up any residual food that may be left in your body from childhood.

What about yoga?

Yoga is OK, but it doesn't count toward your three hours of daily exercise unless you are really sweating.

Try Power Yoga or better yet Bikram Yoga. Power Yoga is very strenuous and burns fat. Bikram Yoga is even more strenuous and burns everything.

Bikram Yoga is the latest Yoga trend involving strenuous exercise done in a room that is heated to at least 100 degrees. You sweat so much, you can lose five pounds in one hour-and-a-half class!

Now that's what we call exercise!

EXERCISE TIPS

Here are five key exercise tips from our resident gym rat:

(1) You should do abdominal exercises every day to achieve that flat stomach that men love. Alternate with a set of 25 sit ups between each set of 12-15 repetitions on the machines at the gym. Three hundred sit-ups are easily achievable given a standard work out time of one hour and 15 minutes. Breathe out very hard and contract the stomach muscles on each up motion. Done incorrectly, sit ups build out your abdominals and actually can add inches to your waste. Do less, if necessary, but do them properly. For every muscle group other than abdominals you must take a day of rest. To keep your program simple alternate legs with back and then a separate day for arms. You can swim every day.

(2) Use lower weights and do more repetitions and sets. But the weights should be heavy enough so that the last few repetitions of each set require serious effort. Otherwise you are just wasting your time and tying up the machines.

(3) Work the large muscle groups first. Typically, the gym will line up the machines this way, so all you have to do is follow them in order.

(4) Yoga is better than the gym. Have you ever seen a fat yoga instructor?

(5) If all else fails, hire a personal trainer. Preferably a good looking guy who will inspire you to get results.

CHAPTER EIGHT

THE GOLD DIGGER'S DIET™

If you are thin and svelte, have no problems, worries or anxieties about food or your diet, don't go up and down in weight, have never weighed more than 125 pounds and haven't purged or starved yourself to lose weight, you can skip this chapter. In fact, if all those things are true you can skip the entire book. You don't need it because you are either superwoman, an android or a teenage boy. The rest of us human females need to watch our weight.

Here's how we do it.

The Diet Doctors

For those of us with mild eating disorders, whose weight occasionally fluctuates above cover-girl norms or who just worry too much about food, we recommend a diet doctor. In Manhattan, Dr. Robert S. Levine and the late Dr. Joseph Greenburg were, until recently, the two diet doctors that Gold Diggers prefer most. Regrettably, Dr. Greenburg recently passed away.

Dr. Levine, who has offices in both Manhattan and Lake Success, New York, tells his patients that, "To mold the body one must first mold the mind."

Although some of Dr. Levine's patients appear to be moulding themselves, there is no question that many of them swear by him. Even men go to him. Comedian Conan O'Brien has been going for years.

The regimens of Dr. Levine and the late Dr. Greenburg both require their patients to eat three meals daily. Each supplement their patients' diet with a healthy compliment of pills, including appetite suppressants (amphetamines). These pills must be taken around mealtimes.

Dr. Levine prohibits all snacking and in between meal eating except for coffee, tea and water. Dr. Greenburg allowed celery and string beans as between meal snacks. Dr. Levine's patient brochure states that mayonnaise and ketchup are never allowed and salt is restricted. He also prohibits diet and no fat products, carbonated beverages, Chinese food, virtually all pasta, rice, butter, bread, whole milk, chicken, turkey roll, fat, sauces, nuts, oil, cheese and yes, alcohol. Things you can eat include tuna packed in water and diet Jell-O. Liver and mixed vegetables are also allowed at dinner.

Both doctors' regimens allow Special K cereal. The principal differences between Dr. Levine and Dr. Greenburg (beside the fact that Dr. Greenburg is dead), is that you only had to see Dr. Greenburg every two weeks and Dr. Greenburg allowed you to drink alcohol. Dr. Levine's patient literature prohibits alcohol (but, if pressed, we hear he won't object to an occasional glass of wine). Since the prospect of eliminating both alcohol and virtually all food from your diet in one fell swoop can be traumatic, the less disciplined among you may wish to try Dr. Greenburg's regimen first. At last report, both doctors were very expensive. Since Dr. Greenburg is dead he may now have a cost advantage. Either way, you will have to stay on your diet until your wedding night.

Let's Face Facts

Rich guys don't marry fat girls. In fact, most men won't even date an overweight woman. If you are serious about landing a rich husband you must get down to your fighting weight.

The good news is that anyone who is serious about it can lose weight. When a single woman comes to us and says "I can't seem to lose weight," our response is always the same.

"Yes, you can!"

Face it, if you are not skinny, you are not going to get desireable dates. Without decent dates, it is going to be difficult to get married. And if you don't get married, you will have to support yourself for the rest of your life.

No matter how skinny you are, your chances of getting married and having children diminish rapidly as you get older. So you don't have a lot of time.

You've got to get skinny now!

If you want to stay single and fat, have another pint of Häagan-Dazs. But if you want to get skinny and marry the rich, get serious about your dieting. You have no time to waste.

It's a matter of lifestyle and death!

Eating Can Kill

The results are now in. The more you eat, the shorter your life span. The human body works most efficiently when it is near starvation. Combine your Gold Digger's Diet™ with our rigorous exercise program. You will become productive and thin. The results will amaze you.

The Less You Eat the Better You'll Feel

Science has now proven that for dozens of species, from mosquitoes to rats to monkeys, caloric restriction leads to longer life and a healthier organism. Reducing caloric intake by 30% increased average life span by one third across numerous species. This is consistent with human studies showing severe life span reductions among seriously overweight people. You may not live to be 150, but you will look and feel 150% better on a rigorous caloric restriction diet.

Inherit Several Fortunes

If you stay on the Gold Digger's Diet™, you could live much longer. This should give you the opportunity to inherit several fortunes.

As it is, nature designed women to outlive their mates to allow us the pleasure of spending money without a husband underfoot to cramp our style. Now with the increased longevity which can result from the Gold Digger's Diet™, you should be able to marry several wealthy men and out-live each of them as they expire before you do from natural causes.

Consider this important piece of Chinese wisdom:

"She who spends last dollar has last laugh."

Of Course You Aren't Too Thin!

Unless you are invisible when you stand sideways, you are not too thin. Generally, if your age plus your weight are a number greater than 165, you are too fat or too old, or both.

Have you looked through *Vogue* recently? Of course you have. The girls are as thin as ever.

Are plus size models in fashion? In a word, no. Not now. Not ever. Plus size models are not models. They are just fat girls with pretty faces who look a bit better than the other fat girls.

Eat Not, Want Not

The less you eat, the less you need to eat. As you eat less and less, your body adjusts to your lower caloric intake. It will become more efficient. It will run at a fever pitch.

To get over the initial hunger pangs when you first start your diet, there are some important Gold Digger's Diet™ aids that can help you soothe your cravings for food.

(1) SELTZER WATER

Carbonated water fills you up with gas which can make you temporarily feel full. This makes some of us feel uncomfortable. For others, the carbon dioxide in seltzer water is a good food substitute. Drink it if it works for you.

(2) COFFEE

Coffee gives you energy. It is also a great laxative. It will help you increase your activity level and decrease your appetite. Have a cup whenever you get hungry. Continue this if it works for you.

(3) ICE

No. Ice is not fattening. It is just frozen water. But you should only make ice from filtered or bottled water to make sure it does not contain any fattening or unhealthy impurities.

(4) CIGARETTES

When you are on a diet, it is not the time to stop smoking. In fact, it is a good time to start smoking.

Nicotine is a great appetite suppressant and energizer. Enjoy your your new addiction as you lose weight. You can always quit after you get married. But don't smoke around your man. Nine times out of ten he won't like it.

(5) Fiber Pills

Fiber pills expand in your body and make you feel full. They are also a good intestinal cleanser. Fiber pills can be an excellent substitute for unhealthy foods.

(6) Amphetamines are a great food

OK, so speed kills. But in the meantime, it can also get you married. Amphetamines suppress your appetite while giving you enormous energy to run around and accomplish important daily tasks, like burning fat. Take them if they work for you, but check with your doctor first.

(7) Chromium Picolinate

Chromium Picolinate assists the body in metabolizing fat. For many people 200 mcg of Chromium Picolinate a day (taken in the morning) may assist with those last stubborn 5 to 6 extra pounds. More is not better. If it is not working for you, or you have any adverse reactions, discontinue use and check with your doctor.

(8) Apple Cider Vinegar and Honey

Take ¼ cup of apple cider vinegar with honey per day. Some people have reported a loss of the desire for fatty foods and a quick loss of 2 to 5 pounds within one to two weeks. But don't drink too much without consulting a physician. Excessive intake of vinegar may have serious implications for your liver. Check with your doctor first.

Appetite Suppressants

Your diet doctor can prescribe appetite suppressants which are very effective in taking your mind off food. Properly prescribed, these drugs can be an invaluable aid to your dieting program. Dr. Levine also recommends co-enzyme Q10 to appropriate patients for "maximum results."

Unfortunately, you will need a prescription. For this, you'll want to line up a few friendly diet doctors. With multiple prescriptions, you should be able to get enough amphetamines to greatly enhance your weight loss program.

If you do enough speed, your entire body will contract in no time. You won't even want to eat!

Yes, speed is psychologically addictive. But, so what? After you are married and leading a life of luxury, you will have plenty of time to give up the addictions that got you thin enough to win that ring from your wealthy husband.

The dangers of the Gold Digger's Diet™ are a necessary evil. And of course we can't be responsible for the possible risks to your health so we advise you to consult with your personal physician before following all of our wise advice. The good news is that you only need the Gold Digger's Diet™ until your wedding day. You can quit the morning after your wedding and binge for the rest of your life! In the meantime, consult your diet doctor and religiously follow what he tells you to do and not to do.

Worry About Self-Esteem After You Are Married

People will whisper that your relentless cycle of dieting and exercise shows that you have low self-esteem. If you are in your 30s and still single, self-esteem may be a luxury you cannot afford. What a true Gold Digger says is that, "If low self-esteem helps me lose weight, I am all for it."

Who We Tell About the Gold Digger's Diet™ is Nobody

The Gold Digger's Diet™ is our secret weapon. We don't talk about it. You wouldn't think about giving nuclear weapons to your worst enemy. Similarly, you do not want to tell anyone about the Gold Digger's Diet™. If your girlfriends, family, therapist or doctor finds out about your diet, they will try to stop you from sticking to it. They will ply you with food, they will follow you around to prevent you from purging, they will say you are sick, they will whisper the "A" word to all your friends.

Remember, your girlfriends have only one motive in getting you off the Gold Digger's Diet™–they want to steal your boyfriend.

Consider the case of Emily. Emily was doing very well on the Gold Digger's Diet™. She was engaged to Brad, a partner at Goldman Sachs who makes almost $10 million a year and is a member of the ultra exclusive Southampton Bathing Corporation.

Her fatal error? She told her best friend Eve about her Gold Digger's Diet™. Eve whispered the "A" word to another girlfriend named

Alexandra who disliked Emily. Alexandra whispered it to Emily's fiancé who began to regard her with suspicion. Eventually Brad caught Emily purging after his birthday dinner at New York's Le Cirque restaurant. Then he found the laxatives and the diet pills. Brad dumped Emily and made her give back the five-carat engagement ring. When Brad dumped her, Emily had a nervous breakdown and went off the Gold Digger's Diet™. Now, Alexandra is married to Brad. Emily weighs 200 pounds and lives on welfare in a rent-controlled apartment in an outer borough.

Never Admit You Were Overweight to Your Boyfriend

Don't talk to your boyfriend about your dieting or how much weight you have lost. He does not want to know about it. If you admit that you were once overweight, he will run screaming in the opposite direction. He knows what all men fear: that a woman who was fat once will be fat again.

The only thing your boyfriend wants to talk about is sex and sports. Your boyfriend wants to assume that you will always be this skinny. He does not want to hear about your weight problem.

PART THREE

Meeting Your Knight
In the Shining Gulf Stream –
High Net Worth Socializing

CHAPTER NINE

THE HIGH NET WORTH DATING CIRCUIT

Go Where the Rich Go

You are not going to marry the rich by sitting at home. To target potential high net worth fiancés, you need to get out and socialize in Manhattan, Southampton, Aspen and Palm Beach. Hit the charity and benefit circuit and high-end cocktail parties without delay. At the big benefits, you can get quickly whisked into the social whirl.

The rich find their mates at parties and through social introductions. All you have to do to meet them is be at the right place, at the right time and stand around looking gorgeous. The men will do the rest themselves.

Find a Partner in Crime

Benefit tickets are expensive. Try to find a male friend or a girlfriend to accompany you to charity events who will pay for his or her own ticket. Better still, find someone so happy to go with you they'll pay for your ticket too. You can help each other meet the people you want. It is difficult to meet people if you are alone at a party. Far better to go with someone who can help arrange introductions. Males who perform this function are called "Walkers."

Never Buy the Dinner Ticket

Dinner tickets for charity parties are very expensive, often costing $500 to $1,000 and up. Buy the dance, dessert or junior or after party ticket instead. No one ever checks to see if you are really a junior! You will avoid the excruciating boredom of sitting at a table of elderly socialites. You will also avoid wearing yourself out through overexposure. Much better to come in fresh after dinner when the wealthy alpha males have a few drinks under their belts. They will be primed and ready to approach you as you make your way through the room on heels in your Chanel skirt.

There are four principal places where you can start your high net worth dating by means of the established benefit circuit: Palm Beach, Aspen, New York and Southampton.

The High Net Worth Dating Circuit

Here is a list of a few high-end charity benefits worth attending on the high net worth dating circuit. Go to all of them.

Manhattan, New York

Metropolitan Museum-Costume Institute Benefit Gala
  (The dinner ticket is $3,500.00; go to the after-party for around $250.00.)

The Frick Museum Winter Ball
  (A beautiful venue and great looking people!)

Museum of Modern Art - Party in the Garden
  (A mixed crowd with some high end attendees.)

New York Academy of Art - Take Home A Nude Party
  (Take home a nude painting from the selection being offered for sale - and a new boyfriend.)

The Museum of the City of New York Summer and Winter Benefit Parties
  (WASPs all the way!)

The New York Athletic Club - Night of Aphrodite
(The men switch tables so you get a new man with every course!)

The Metropolitan Foundation Fall Party at the Central Park Boathouse
(Uninhibited, easy-to-meet crowd.)

The TriBeCa Ball
(Elite artsy crowd.)

The Save Venice Winter Ball
(High end Euro crowd.)

The Metropolitan Museum–Apollo Circle Junior Party in The Temple of Dendur
(Excellent crowd, but lots of female competition.)

The Whitney Museum–Junior Whitney Contemporaries
(Lower end mixed social and art crowd.)

The International Neuroscience Foundation Benefit
(The good, the bad, and the ugly.)

The New York Studio School Annual Benefit
(Established art scene.)

The Tibet House Annual Benefit
(Look for the Uma Thurman Family, David Bowie and Richard Gere.)

Opening of the TriBeCa Film Festival
(Cinemaphiles and minor celebrities.)

The Winter Antiques Show–Young Collectors Night
(Wasps and beautiful people.)

The Museum of Natural History Winter Ball
(The dinner is in the Whale Room–but go to the after-party.)

The Inwood House Annual Winter Benefit
(Katie Couric usually emcees)

The Princess Grace Foundation Fall Benefit
(Euro and WASP Society Folk. The Pre-parties can be as good as the actual event.)

The Central Park Nature Conservancy Halloween Ball
(Very high end society and movers and shakers)

The Hamptons

The Guild Hall–Junior Benefit

Group for the South Fork

The Parrish Museum of Southampton–Annual Benefit
(Watch out for Toxic Bachelors in the after dinner crowd.)

Taste of the Hamptons

Chefs and Champagne Benefit of The James Beard Foundation

Southampton Hospital Benefit

Robert Wilson Watermill Arts Foundation Benefit

Phoenix House Benefit

Ovarian Cancer Benefit

Planned Parenthood Annual Benefit

Anything at the Wolfer Estate (Wine Vineyards)

Any Hamptons Magazine or Hamptons Cottages and Gardens party

The Hamptons Film Festival–Closing Party (in October)

Anything at Aerin Lauder's, Alec Baldwin's, Howard Oxenburg's or Kathy Hilton's house and most parties on Southhampton's Gin Lane or Ox Pasture Road

Any HBO and other Film premieres
(Skip the films and go to the after-parties, if you can find out where they are.)

Palm Beach

The Red Cross–New Year's Eve Ball

Juvenile Diabetes Benefit

The Coconut Ball

The Preservation Foundation of Palm Beach

The Cystic Fibrosis Foundation Benefit

The American Heart Foundation Association Ball

The Scottish Highlands Ball

The Winter Antique Show Annual Outdoor Art Show

Anything at the houses of Martin Gruss, The Fanjul's, Pauline Pitt, Howard
    Oxenburg, The Picketts, The Lauders, The du Ponts, The Guests,
    The Perelmans, The Bronfmans, Wilbur Ross, Nelson Peltz or
    Donald Trump.

Once you have been to a half dozen or so of these events in each location, you will get invitations to most of the rest. Some of the benefits we have mentioned are very expensive, so put them on your credit card, or someone else's. The tickets will just be one more debt for your husband to pay off after you are married.

If you are really uncomfortable paying for or running up huge debts to pay for benefit tickets, you can try to figure out how to crash them. Morgan Peabody, III has written a helpful guide to getting into parties for free called *How to Get in Anywhere – The Expert's Guide to Party Crashing.* You can use his techniques to get into almost any party or event in almost any location. (See back section of this book for further information.)

Go in as Arm Candy

Attending a benefit or party on the arm of a handsome "Walker" is a great way in the door. You generally won't have to pay for your ticket because your date wants you there to show off on his arm.

The disadvantage is that you will have to flirt discreetly with other men. Potential suitors may also be reluctant to talk to you if you are obviously with a date. Try to find reasons to wander around the party on your own. Usually you will find a girlfriend there whom you can use as an excuse to get away from your "date". Of course, the ideal situation is attending with a date who is at the party to find other women himself. Together you can work-the-room and help each other meet girls and guys. You should explicitly agree on this approach before you go to the party so that you avoid misunderstandings and are focused and efficient once you get inside.

Do Your Homework

There is no face book for the rich. There are no trading cards for single high net worth men. You have to do your homework to know who the rich are, where they live and get a general impression of their past and present entanglements. Gossiping with society women is an excellent way to get the real dope on the available High Net Worth Men.

You do not want to go to a party, chat with a circle of guests and find out later that one of them was one of Rupert Murdoch's heirs. You need this information in real time. If you don't know who someone is or you missed the introduction, discreetly ask them again. Find out who they are, where they live and where they grew up. Get the last name.

The rich and well-known often introduce themselves using only their first name. This means one of three things. They assume you know who they are, they don't care whether you know who they are or they don't want you to know who they are. Whatever the reason, it is your job to get his last name.

Business Cards are Gold Mines of Information

A man will often give you his business card and ask you to contact him. Of course you are not going to do that. What you are going to do is use the business card to research him. Go to his firm's web site. Find out what his business is. Look for his biography on his company web site. You will often find his age and education, including schools and years attended. If it is a law firm, you can look up the profits per partner in the *American Lawyer Magazine's* annual survey. If he is a banker, look for his title. If he is a Managing Director at Morgan Stanley or elsewhere, he almost certainly meets your net worth and income standards. Then search the internet for other references. You can find any news article that mentions him and you will often be able to determine whether or not he is married, as well as public information about previous divorces, if any.

After doing your reseach, if you like what you find, arrange to meet him again by attending social functions he might be at or send him an e-mail with a business question. It is rarely necessary to call him on the phone. If he is interested, he will pursue your opening.

CHAPTER TEN

MEETING A HIGH NET WORTH MAN

Regrettably, you will not be able to marry your man unless you meet him first. This means you are going to have to get off your tushy and do some work.

Many men will pursue you at the slightest opening. The faintest hint of a glance or smile. Sometimes they will even approach you from behind unexpectedly and with no encouragement at all.

However, these highly aggressive guys might not be the ones you want to meet. In fact, many of them will turn out to be toxic bachelors. The rest of the pack may need some encouragement. Sometimes a smile and a long look in his direction will suffice. Other times you will have to say something to start a conversation. Remember that many wealthy men are socially awkward. From your perspective, the more awkward they are the better. The less social skills they have, the less likely they are to meet other beautiful women and the more dependent they will be on you.

It usually does not take much to get the ball rolling. A man's primary purpose at a party is generally to meet women. Business and social contacts are usually secondary considerations.

What you say doesn't matter. But it should not seem forced or artificial. Here are seven simple openings you can use. Use them with a smile.

OPENING LINES

(1) Nice tie!

(2) Great party!

(3) It's packed in here!

(4) What are you having? (at the bar or indicating to his drink).

(5) It's a bit chilly! (maybe he'll take the initiative and cover your shoulders with his jacket).

(6) Great band! (don't say this unless there is one).

(7) Wonderful flowers! (find anything about the décor to comment on in a positive way).

Always be positive. "This party sucks" or "where did they find these triple ZZZ list losers" may not go over well. Particularly if you are talking to the host, a friend of the host, someone on the event committee or some moron who just thinks it's a good party.

The current smoke-free environment has deprived us of the traditional quest for a cigarette or a match as an opener. And indicating how desperate you are for a cigarette is no longer universally regarded as a positive way to strike up a conversation.

Watch the flow of people through the party. Position yourself so you can catch your target's eye as he goes by. Or wait until he moves to the bar to get a drink. Then follow him and try to stand beside him so he sees you. Use a simple opener or, if you are lucky, he may ask if he can get you a drink.

Once you begin talking, if he likes you, he will go into autopilot. He will begin his campaign to get your phone number. Once he has your phone number he will generally begin strategizing on how to get you into bed.

Guess what?

You're in business!

Moving the Place Cards

Disappointed at the seating arrangement at a large sit-down dinner party or charity benefit? Did you find yourself seated next to an old geezer who has been married so long he is deaf in both hairy ears? Switching name cards with someone more desirably situated is an easy solution to this dreadful problem. Being seated at the wrong table can mean a total loss of social opportunities and an expensive evening wasted. Move a competitor's name card to your seat and put yours at hers. Immediately befriend everyone else at the table. If the person figures out she has been moved, you can simply say, "Oh Charles and I are such old friends and we are so looking forward to sitting together." Hopefully the person you moved was not Charles' date for the evening.

Opportunistic Seating

Another way out of social purgatory is to wait until everyone else has been seated. Now scan the unoccupied chairs for the places next to potential targets. Sit down in the choicest unoccupied seat you can find. Don't worry, between 10% and 20% of the guests at large dinners and benefits do not show up. So the chances are you will be able to enjoy your dinner in your new location. In the unlikely event someone tries to claim your seat, you can always graciously apologize or explain with frustration that someone is sitting in your seat. Then move to another seat at a table that you like.

The opportunistic seating technique can also be used effectively in crashing large summer benefit parties as explained in Morgan Peabody, III's invaluable guide, *How To Get In Anywhere: The Expert's Guide To Party Crashing*. Arrive after everyone else has sat down and circle the tent from the outside until you come to the temporary lavatory facilities. Go into the ladies room and then emerge and walk boldly into the party as though you had just left. Tickets or wrist-bands are almost never checked for people returning from the bathroom, except at Bridgehampton Polo where they are, unfortunately, on to this little gimmick.

Fending Off the Competition

The easiest way to fend off a competing Gold Digger is to make her motives known to your target and all his friends. Every time your competitor's name comes up, refer to her as "a Gold Digger from way back" or "an Old-Timer". Insinuate that her last bit of plastic surgery was botched causing her to look like a "death's head under ultraviolet light." Or, insinuate that she has a "serious eating disorder." Be sure to mention these items to one or two of your girlfriends, but ask them to keep the information confidential. Within 48 hours everyone you know will have heard all about her.

Your Gold Digging is Our Secret

Never discuss your goals and motives with anyone. The only thing that can keep you from your goal of marrying a rich man is someone else's knowledge of it. Beware of your girlfriends. If your target finds out or even suspects that you are out for cash, you will be excised from his life long before you ever learn which girl "friend" ratted you out.

Of course, your acquaintances may speculate that you are looking for the big score but you must never say anything that would confirm their suspicions. Always say you are looking for true love. Any unguarded statement can spread like the plague and kill your chances for a successful operation. Other women will happily undermine you by repeating anything you say or do that smells of gold digging to everyone they know. They may even make scandalous things up about you. This tactic is designed to eliminate you from the field of play.

You Deserve Success!

The ambitious woman who is focused, strategically minded and pays attention to her appearance deserves to land her high net worth man. Don't be intimidated by anyone. Every gorgeous, charming woman you meet on the high net worth circuit is just another girl until she is married. You have just as much chance as she does of marrying a rich man. Everything else being more or less equal, the more determined woman will always win.

Let's say you are at a cocktail party and the man you want is chatting with Patricia Duff. Patricia Duff is a celebrity, a great beauty and a veteran of the high net worth dating wars. But since she divorced Ron Perelman, the truth is, she is just another single girl. And a girl with baggage at that. Your target is going to think more than twice about getting involved with her. He may even think about it six times, but most likely he isn't going to go there.

If you are dealing with a high profile conversational competitor, wait for the slightest lull in the conversation, then go up and join them. These lulls sometimes occur right before the man is about to ask for your competitor's phone number. Most likely when you approach, your celebrity competitor will wander off in search of other prey (after all she won't have any interest in talking to you). And if you have moved quickly enough, he won't have had time to get her phone number.

Of course, he may ignore you completely, but that too is good intelligence. Don't take it personally. Some men won't look at you if they are talking to a celebrity. They focus all their energy on the celebrity. This is a form of high-end ass kissing. If you sense this is going on, wait until your high profile opponent has left before you approach. Your target will likely spill the beans on everything she told him.

Convert to Judaism

Two of the greatest gold diggers of all time did just that -- Marilyn Monroe (for Arthur Miller) and Patricia Duff (for Ron Perelman).

It shows your man how much you care that you'll go to such lengths to please him. Hebrew lessons, weekly meetings with the Rabbi, spiritual cleansing baths–it takesover eight months. This gives you just enough time to complete the conversion process before the wedding.

Remember That Men Are Like Buses

Whatever happens, don't get discouraged and never take rejection personally. Remember that men are like buses. You don't need to run after them. After a while another one always comes along.

Chapter Eleven

THE BACKGROUND CHECK

Sure you can hire Kroll Associates to investigate and tail your target 24 hours a day, seven days a week. You can have his friends and business colleagues discreetly interrogated, you can have his bank accounts and financial assets investigated, his résumé checked out and the validity of his divorces confirmed. But hiring a private investigator to thoroughly investigate your man will cost you plenty. From $20,000 to $200,000 or even more. And you still might miss something.

As previously explained, the best way to vet your guy's background is to do it yourself on the cheap and on the sly. Start with the basics. Google him. Then Google his firm. Better still, run a thorough Lexis/Nexis check (this is a special paid search service that should cost about $40.00 Follow up any leads that come up. Run similar checks on his ex-wives, children and best friends. Then start inquiring about his business reputation. Do he and his firm pay their bills on time? Any SEC investigations or lawsuits? Is Eliot Spitzer after him? Any hints of scandal in his family background? What comes up on his ex-girlfriends? Who are they? Was he ever gay?

One enterprising gold digger we know was happily dating a highly respected, recently divorced U.S. Senator. She located press reports detailing meager assests and his first wife's small divorce settlement thanks to a few minutes of due diligence. The moral of this story is: powerful positions and prestige don't necessarily come with cash.

Ask him about his recent ex-girlfriends. Get their names. If he still includes them in his social circle, take them aside and casually and discreetly pump them for all relevant information. Ask them what happened between them and him. Most women will spill their guts about a high profile ex to any willing listener. Why did they break up with him? What did he say about marriage and children? Was he stingy? Angry? Depressed? An alcoholic or a drug user? Any terminal or sexually transmitted diseases? What were his worst habits? How was his gift giving? Did he appear to be in any financial trouble? Any ex girlfriend who kept popping up? What does his Hamptons house look like inside? Who decorated his apartment in New York? How good is the landscaping in the country house? Is that plane owned or leased?

You get the idea.

CHAPTER TWELVE

THE SENIOR CIRCUIT –
THE OLD, THE RICH
AND THE BUTT-UGLY

It's time to define your target on the High Net Worth Social Circuit. Pure gold.

How do you know you have struck gold?

Check to see how many of the following five characteristics your man possesses.

(1) HE SHOULD BE RICH.

He must meet the Minimum Net Wealth Standard. Hello! this goes without saying. Smart, rich men don't mind being liked for their money. "Better to be liked for something I have, than something I don't," is the attitude of the smart, rich man.

(2) HE SHOULD BE OLD.

Old means less options. He does not have time to waste looking for women.

(3) HE SHOULD BE BUTT-UGLY.

Handsome and rich men are spoiled by women. They are likely to be narcissistic which means they won't bond well with others. In fact, they bond best with themselves. You want someone who appreciates the fact that you are with him. Someone who feels that you like him for him, notwithstanding his butt-ugliness. Of course, don't tell him it's for his money. To some he might look butt-ugly. But you know better. He looks damn good when he's standing on his wallet.

(4) HE SHOULD BE INSECURE.

This is a key characteristic of a good husband. While your mogul may be outwardly the very picture of self-confidence, his personal vanity and his insecurity may make him needy and jealous. His insecurities provide a marvelous array of tools that you can use to control him. Self-confident, emotionally healthy men are best avoided because they will not bond with you. They will only bond well with other emotionally healthy people. You will not get any money out of the emotionally healthy man because he does not need you. The neurotic man on the other hand can be a source of constant joy, attention and cash. He tries to win you with cash because he is unsure of his ability to do so as a man.

(5) HE SHOULD STILL BE WORKING.

Super-successful men tend to work until they drop. They just don't know what else to do. Beware of someone who is retired or talks about retirement. Retirement means you are out of the game. More importantly for you, it means he will have too much time on his hands. You are not going to want him under your feet in the house all day while you are trying to work out with your personal trainer and make spa appointments and lunch dates with your friends. The big risk is that the more time you spend with him, the more time he has to find out you are a gold digger. And the more time you spend together the more it will be like being married, usually not a plus for a man. Marriages break up because the couple spends too much time together as often as they break up because the couple spends not enough time together. You want a guy who is still working. A man who has limited time will appreciate spending it with you. A man like this won't have enough time to hunt for other women.

If your guy has all five of these characteristics get him to the altar fast, before someone else does. If he has any four you are in pretty good shape, unless of course he is missing *número uno* (the money).

The Senior Circuit

For those of you who are over 35 or already in your 40s or even 50s, there are many lucrative opportunities available on the senior circuit. In many ways the senior circuit is where the real gold is. On the senior circuit, cash is easier to come by.

The senior circuit is generally populated by men who are sixty and over although there are a smattering of more desirable men in their late 50s.

You will know immediately when you enter a senior circuit party by the sea of white hair and bald heads. Many will be married but there will also be a mix of old, single, wealthy guys. High net worth guys who don't feel comfortable operating amongst the younger set.

The good thing about the senior circuit is that you won't see any models and very few of the late 20s, early 30s gold diggers that you have to compete with at events for the younger set. On the senior circuit you can compete well into your 50s as an attractive and polished older woman. We call these women "Silver Sirens". Silver Sirens are in great demand at important senior benefits.

The parties are slower paced, better dressed and if you are used to the action and energy of the younger set, a bit boring. And this is another important advantage of the senior circuit, because it can help you to make a big impression.

A nice leggy 35-year-old blond in high heels and a little black dress will turn all the heads at a senior circuit party. At a typical charity event or on the junior circuit there may be several dozen single women as impressive or better looking than you. On the senior circuit there are likely to be only one or two. The older men will be clamoring for your attention. And there is still plenty of room for the older woman to operate as a Silver Siren. Remember to be a little bit subtle. Go with an older male friend you are not involved with and work-the-room together. He can also help you make introductions and identify and avoid the real players, who are likely to be the first guys to approach you at the party.

Why Are There so Few of the Younger Gold Diggers on the Senior Circuit?

Tickets to senior circuit events tend to run $500 to $1,000 per person. This shuts out attractive women who don't have that kind of money. And most younger women would be bored at such an event anyway. After all, they are looking for someone closer to their own age. Always a mistake for the truly ambitious woman. If you can't find an old geezer to spring for your ticket, just sneak into the party. Few women attempt to sneak into the older benefits. And security is often very lax. You can just claim to be a social reporter for a glossy magazine that is covering the event. You shouldn't have any problem if you look the part and speak with confidence.

Once you are in, don't waste a second, work the room!!!

You can usually find a sexy older guy to flirt with in seconds. Older men will be less fearful of approaching you, more charming in manner and less reluctant to part with cash than their younger counterparts. But watch out for the womanizers!

Of course, you don't have to marry a 92-year-old billionaire like Anna Nicole Smith. But do look for bald guys. If you are lucky and they are single, it could be a sign that they are on chemotherapy. A fast moving girl can sometimes get married and get hubby's Will changed before cancer takes him into the great beyond.

It is sometimes convenient to have a spouse who can walk, eat and go to the bathroom all by himself. And there are plenty of wealthy guys in their 70s and 80s who can still get to the bathroom unassisted.

Remember that although the oldsters are as desperate for sex as a younger guy, their advances will be easier to repel. They know they are starting from a weak bargaining position by asking a much younger woman to sleep with them. This will make them more likely to part with gifts and cash to make up for the age imbalance.

Going out on the senior circuit, while not always ideal, offers wonderful opportunity for the still single woman in her late 30s and 40s and yes, even 50s.

These men will have already had their children and they are unlikely to want more. They want to have fun and they are usually willing to pay for it.

Here's where to find them.

The Senior Circuit–Events

The Southamptons

Southampton Hospital annual benefit
LongHouse Reserve summer gala (East Hampton)
Phoenix House Benefit (usually at Bob Hurst's house, Sagaponac)
The Group for the South Fork
The Nature Conservancy benefit
Anything at: the Bathing Corporation, the Meadow Club or Southampton
　　　Bath and Tennis Club

Palm Beach

Red Cross Ball (New Year's Eve)
Every other party in Palm Beach.

Aspen

Almost every party in Aspen has its share of wealthy single oldsters.
They may not look like Brad Pitt, but the cash will definitely be there.

Manhattan

Metropolitan Museum of Art–Costume Institute Benefit Gala
　　(This is a crossover event, lots of younger celebrities and plenty of old
　　money too–but to really take advantage of it you will have to get
　　someone to shell out $3,500 for the dinner ticket. The after-party ranges
　　from $250-$300 depending on the year.)
Winter Antiques Show Opening Party at the Park Avenue Armory
　　(attracts the older social set; there is also a younger, less expensive,
　　but still glamorous, event for the "young collectors").

　　　In Manhattan, eligible oldsters are often part of established WASP
society. New York City is a playground for wealthy men but they tend to
hang out with younger people. So you can also find them at the
mainstream charity functions.

Chapter Thirteen

WALKERS AND GIGOLOS

Thank God For Walkers

Walkers (known as "cabin boys" in the South) are a common sight in the High Net Worth dating world. They are presentable males who will take you into an important party or event. If you are lucky, they will pay for your ticket. Walkers have their own reasons for being at the party and they are delighted to have you as arm candy at their side. But you must be careful in choosing your Walker so that appearing with him does not sully your reputation.

Walkers should have the following characteristics:

(1) They should be from a good (if not prominent) family.

(2) They should look good in a tux or a blue blazer, as the occasion demands.

(3) They should be well-mannered and gracious at all times.

(4) They should not pretend they own you. They must be helpful and positive when you make it clear to another guest that you are not dating your Walker.

(5) They should be discreet enough in their flirtations not to embarrass you.

(6) They should pick you up at your place, get you drinks at the party when you are not busy with other targets and, if desired, drop you at home after it is over.

(7) They should pay for things as though you were on a normal date.

(8) They should discreetly introduce you to eligible males.

(9) They should not stand too near when you are flirting with another man.

(10) They should look dignified and in control at all times.

Needless to say, good Walkers are in great demand. If you can't land a good Walker, take a gay one. Gay Walkers do it for the social credibility of going out with a woman. Gay Walkers are no mess and no fuss. But to avoid embarrassment they should be discreetly gay. Raving queens may repel the type of man you want to meet.

Gigolos

Gigolos are the male equivalent of a gold digger. A Gigolo is no substitute for a good Walker.

With a Gigolo, the world is upside down. Gigolos are men who expect you to pay for them. (Ridiculous as it may seem, such men actually do exist.) The profession thrives in sunny and fashionable resorts. Palm Beach in winter is a haven for Gigolos.

Gigolos are not difficult to spot. They are the young, handsome guy with the rich, older woman. You know you are with a Gigolo if you paid for his benefit ticket.

Just Say No to the Gigolo

Gigolos are not good marriage prospects. And they are always low net worth individuals. Going out with them will irreparably damage your reputation. If one of your girlfriends finds out that you paid a man for sex, the news will be all over the country in minutes.

Gigolos. Don't go there!

CHAPTER FOURTEEN

SOUTHAMPTON – SUMMER MONEYFEST

For many years now, almost whenever a new business titan or media celebrity with any East Coast connections emerges in the public eye, one of the first things he or she does is buy a house in the Hamptons. This irresistible impulse has made the Hamptons into some of the most valuable real estate on the planet.

Southampton is the center of the Hamptons summer moneyfest. Both the old money and the new money is there. Southampton attracts more social and business wealth than East Hampton or Bridgehampton and is the center of the most frenetic charitable event season on Earth. There are four or five major benefit parties almost every weekend from Memorial Day through Labor Day and numerous smaller ones that are also well-attended and covered in the media. In addition, there are huge society garden parties, beach parties, promotional events, store parties, fashion parties, movie premieres, after-parties, pre-parties, weddings, singles parties, dinner parties and occasionally raucous sex parties with swinging or S&M as the theme. The focus is on fun and you can spend most every summer weekend floating from one $100,000 plus party or event to the next and many of these are at private homes with tents and hundreds of guests.

The best Hamptons benefits for finding high net worth guys are listed below. Watch for them carefully. You never know which one your future husband may be hunting for you at.

The Best Hamptons Benefits

The Guild Hall Junior Benefit
(younger glamour crowd; but the party is hit or miss)

Group for the South Fork
(established WASP set)

The Parrish Museum of Southampton Annual Benefit
(watch out for Toxic Bachelors in the after dinner crowd.)

The James Beard Foundation Chefs and Champagne Benefit
(glamour foodies and glitteratti)

Southampton Hospital Benefit
(old line society)

Taste of the Hamptons
(more single foodies, but younger and less glam)

Robert Wilson Watermill Arts Foundation Benefit
(very high end art crowd, loaded with celebrities)

Phoenix House Benefit
(a mixed bag. Roy Scheider always goes)

Ovarian Cancer Benefit
(not a bad party for such an awful disease)

Love Heals–Beach Bash Benefit
(a good younger crowd to work)

Planned Parenthood Annual Benefit
(the party is not much more inspiring than the subject)

Anything at the Wolfer Estate
(but don't date the charming German owner)

Any Hamptons Magazine or Hamptons Cottages and Gardens party
(Hamptons Mag has a younger crowd)

The closing party for the Hamptons Film Festival
(often packed with celebs)

Anything at: Aerin Lauder's, Alec Baldwin's, Howard Oxenburg's or Kathy Hilton's house and most parties on Gin Lane or Ox Pasture Road

Any HBO Films premiere
(skip the film and go to the after-party.)

For the literary set go to the celebrity readings at 5 p.m. every Saturday at the Book Hampton Store in East Hampton

Restaurants

As in most resorts the restaurant season is always changing but a few select fixtures have established themselves on the high net worth dating circuit.

Mirko's. This is the WASP business bastion for power dinners. Hidden away behind the post office in Watermill, Mirko's draws Southampton's old money and business power brokers. Unfortunately, there is no bar scene to speak of. So you have to go there for dinner and try to table hop.

Red Bar. The glamour restaurant in Southampton is the Red Bar. Co-owner David Lowenburg was one of the founders of School Street, the pick-up scene restaurant in Bridgehampton. The Red Bar has a small bar scene and a fashionable high-end clientele. Hang out at the bar on Friday or Saturday night and see what develops.

George Martins. This newbie wood-paneled steakhouse in Southampton Village often has an older bar scene ranging from local kids to aging socialites. It's hit or miss but worth an occasional visit.

Savannah. Located near the Southampton train station, this lovely restaurant has a good bar scene especially on Friday evenings when the WASP investment banking contingent stops in on the way home from the city to their Southampton estates.

The American Hotel. A fine restaurant with an extraordinary wine list and a historic location, this Sag Harbor classic attracts a diverse crowd of celebrities, old money, singles, writers and fashion people as well as plain old tourists and day trippers. The bar scene can be so active on a summer Saturday that the line to get in goes out into the street. Sit outside and smile at the high net worth men as they go by.

Nick and Toni's. This is the top celebrity Mecca in East Hampton Yes, you will see Steven Spielberg, Ron Perelman, Martha Stewart (when she gets out), Billy Joel and Robert De Niro sitting in "Power Alley", the row of six tables between the maître d'hôtel stand and the wood burning stove. There is a small bar scene here although most people are having dinner. Reservations are always difficult.

Stephen Talkhouse. Great old-time bands and high net worth socializing for the younger set characterize this popular Amagansett institution run by Peter Hornerkamp. The cover charge when there is entertainment keeps out the undesireables.

Nightlife

In general the late night nightlife in the clubs is for the younger set, although you will find forty-plus bankers and toxic bachelors of all persuasions frequenting these crowded hotspots. Beware of drinking and driving. The cops in the Hamptons generally, and in Southampton, in particularly, are very tough and vigilant and they target the clubs. On a Saturday night in summer they seem to be everywhere. If possible have a designated driver who is not drinking or drinking minimally.

Nightlife places change hands almost every season but they are always in the same locations and they are always run by Manhattan club owners/promoters who follow the money East in summer. Don't go to these places unless you frequent them in Manhattan and know the promoters. But if you get dragged there, know what you are in for.

In Southampton, there is the *Tavern*, a large space on Tuckahoe Lane off the Montauk Highway that gets going late and keeps going until 4 A.M. *Jet East* on Noyac Road caters to the fashion crowd but some nights end up looking like a BBQ (Brooklyn, Bronx & Queens) fest. *Conscience Point Inn* died out after the Lizzie Grubman fiasco and the town bought it to ensure no more late night clubs would occupy the space. The bar on Water street in Sag Harbor (formerly *Rocco's*) is mobbed and sweaty with lots of Bridge and Tunnel action (no high-end gold digging here). The *Star Room*, in Wainscott between Bridgehampton and East Hampton, gets a mixed crowd, including some glitteratti. In East Hampton, *Resort* on Three Mile Harbor Road veers between the BBQ and fashion crowds.

The Clubs

The Hamptons super exclusive private clubs still play an important but not dominant role in Hamptons social life, particularly among the WASP old guard. The three most exclusive WASP clubs are the Southampton Bathing Corporation, The Meadow Club and, in East Hampton, the stately and venerable Maidstone Club. For people who are merely rich and successful, Southampton Bath & Tennis provides an option, even if you are Jewish. Meeting the members isn't hard. Just put on your sexiest bikini and plant yourself on the beach right in front of the Bathing Corp. After the preppy millionaires get tired of watching you they are likely to invite you in for a drink. You can accomplish the same thing at Bath & Tennis and the Maidstone Club by sitting in front of the clubhouse. This can be easily accomplished since there is public parking near all three beach clubs and the clubs are forbidden from excluding anyone from the beach. One thing these clubs share besides the usual social backbiting, jealous wives and spoiled children is an absence of attractive women. However, these clubs are very useful in accumulating high net worth men in one easy to find geographic location that you can sunbathe in front of. So get out the suntan lotion and pick out a bikini that will ensure your life of leisure.

Trolling for Cocktail Parties

If you have been living like a hermit and haven't been invited to any cocktail parties and don't have a benefit ticket on a summer Saturday, do not despair. Just get in the car with your girlfriend and drive along Gin Lane or Ox Pasture Road in Southampton or Lily Pond Lane in East Hampton starting around 5:30 in the afternoon. Look for groupings of 20 or more cars. *Voila!* You have found your cocktail party! Saunter in on high heels and you will both be warmly welcomed by the males at the party.

CHAPTER FIFTEEN

PALM BEACH – ROCOCO GOLD DIGGING

Gold Digging Central

As you work the high net worth dating circuit in Manhattan and Southampton, you will undoubtedly meet a number of people who spend some or much of their winter on a tiny 3.75 square mile Island off the coast of Florida. This island is, of course Palm Beach, the third and southernmost point of what is often reffered to as the lucrative "Bermuda Triangle" (Manhattan–Southampton–Palm Beach).

Palm Beach is an international center of the over-the-top, spend more than the other guy, excess. There are few, if any, other places on Earth more jammed with billionaires and multi-millionaires than Palm Beach. Wildly extravagant interiors, insanely expensive shopping and more jewelry stores per permanent resident than any other community on Earth.

Unfortunately, Palm Beach hosts among the most competitive older gold digging scenes you can find. The ratio of women to high net worth men is extraordinarily high. On the other hand, the ratio of high net worth men to men generally is also very high and there is a discernable lack of younger women. You can operate effectively here as a Silver Siren. The first thing you will notice in Palm Beach is that it is an older crowd. Effectively it is all senior circuit all the time. If you are an attractive younger woman in the 30-40 range who is willing to date the 60 plus man, you can easily outplay the competition by emphasizing your sleek unenhanced good looks.

Palm Beach is also the plastic surgery capital of the Eastern United States. It is rare to see a woman who hasn't had a nip and tuck. Most women over 40 have been reshaped (and occasionally disfigured) by cosmetic surgery. Some local men joke that Palm Beach women have air bags in their breasts which they inflate on arriving in Florida and deflate on the flight back to New York.

Private clubs have a larger role in Palm Beach social life than in Southampton or Aspen. The principal clubs are the *Bath and Tennis*, *Everglades* and *Sailfish* clubs and the *Palm Beach Country Club*. B&T and Everglades are WASP bastions. More non-WASP members are found at the other clubs, at Mar-a-Lago and for those who can't get in elsewhere, the club at the Breakers. Further north is the super-WASPY, hyper low key *Jupiter Island Club*. *Club Collette* is a private dinner club for the geezer and plastic surgery set. While Club Collette tried to make a go of it in Southampton a few years back, they failed to charge enough money for memberships to attract a strong high net worth clientele.

To get oriented, fish for older men at the bar at *Bice* (313½ Worth Avenue), *Taboo* (221 Worth Avenue), *Café L'Europe* (331 South County Road) or *Echo* (230 Sunrise Avenue). *Cucina* (257 Royal Poinciana) is the place for the younger crowd. Better yet try to identify a local Walker to take you into the private clubs. Understand that Walkers are in greater demand here due to the shortage of males generally. Anyone named Ramsey will generally do the trick.

One of the key advantages of Palm Beach nightlife (such as it is) is the absence of women under 35. Young people simply cannot afford and are not old enough to have inherited a house in Palm Beach. Even the hookers tend to be over 35. Except at *Cucina*, the only young people you see are the children of the super rich and the occasional native. As a younger, desirable woman you will have a wide open field in Palm Beach. All you need is a friend with a place to stay. A 10 day stay between Christmas and New Year's Day should yield numerous divorced prospects. If you are a very beautiful young woman it will be like shooting billionaires in a barrel. But be careful, gossip travels fast. If you blow your cover here word will get back to New York before you do.

The official high season is Thanksgiving through March 1st, and the busiest time is the week between Christmas and New Year's Day. Numerous high net worth parties take place during this frantic week. The security at these high-end cash bashes ranges from non-existent to porous. A determined girl can often just sail past the check-in and walk right on into the big New Year's benefits.

The New Year's Eve party given by the *Coconut Club* is worth attending. A gap in the fence on the street 100 feet toward the ocean from the *Colony Hotel* provides an easy walk-in entrance. Otherwise work your way in the back entrance or read a name from the list at the front and claim to be that person. At the *Red Cross Ball* (which is generally held at The Breakers), work your way in from the back bar which adjoins the rear entrance to the party.

The Palm Beach circuit tends to be cliquish and exclusionary. Anti-Semitism is among the principal industries in Palm Beach ranked only slightly behind gossip, golf, tennis, alcoholism and lounging by the pool. Anti-Semitism is particularly widely practiced in the private clubs. The Everglades Club once refused to seat Estée Lauder for lunch because she is Jewish.

Pet Society

For an over-the-top experience, pick up a copy of *Palm Beach Pet Society*, a glossy magazine with pictures of the top dogs (literally) in Palm Beach. For those interested in human mates, *Palm Beach Society* magazine will give you a monthly facebook of who's who among the old guard. They also publish annually *Palm Beach Power & Glory* which gives valuable information and photos of Palm Beach's high net worth denizens, including valuable lists of SWORDS (single, widowed or recently divorced men).

The top Palm Beach party givers are listed below:

Top Palm Beach Hosts and Hostesses

Conrad Black
Ariana and Dixon Boardman
Stephanie Seymour and Peter Brant
Joanne de Guardiola
Beth Rudin Dewoody
Richard Ekstract
Pepe Fanjul
Celia Lipton Farris
Kate Ford
Martin and Audrey Gruss
George Hamilton
Veronica Heart
Carl Icahn
Kelly Klein
David and Julia Koch
Terry Allen Kramer
Leonard and Evelyn Lauder
Carol and Earl Mack
Dina Merrill
Damon Mezzacappa
Howard and Nadia Oxenburg
Ron Perelman
Carroll Petrie
Robin and John Pickett
Pauline Pitt
Marjorie Gubelman and Reze Raein
Billy and Kathy Rayner
Wilbur Ross and Hilary Geary
Alfred and Judy Taubman
Donald Trump

If you get an invitation from any of them, go to the party! If you hear about any of these parties but you are not invited, try to crash them.

Palm Beach is filled with stories of high-end gold digging excess. One long suffering eastern European wife ran through the halls of the Biltmore residences screaming "free at last, free at last!" when her husband unexpectedly passed away. Her husband had bought numerous benefit tickets before his late fall demise. Not wanting to miss these important (and prepaid) social opportunities, his widow instructed the funeral home "to keep him on ice until spring." At which point she shipped him back to Yugoslavia for the funeral.

CHAPTER SIXTEEN

ASPEN –
IT'S NOT ABOUT THE SKIING

The ski season at Aspen brings together the greatest concentration of celebrity and high net worth socializing on the planet. The celebrity egos are so big here that some call it "Ass-Pen." And many of them are so old you can call it "Has-Been." Because Aspen is so small, all you have to do is go there and wangle a place to stay and you will find yourself in the middle of an over-the-top social frenzy like no other.

The best times to be there are over Christmas and New Year's, the President's Day weekend and Easter. Every moment in Aspen at these times is a golden opportunity, so look your best every time you leave your room or even look out the window.

The top hotels are very expensive. A room at *The Little Nell* during peak season can set you back $800 a night. The best approach is to rent a condominium with a few girlfriends. Try the Frias real estate agency. They seem to have a good range of options.

The peak of the high net worth mating season in Aspen runs from December 26 through January 1. Then, just as suddenly the frenzy is over as the social crowd flies back from whence it came. From attending two or three parties every night, from the 26th until New Year's Eve, the hapless socialite may find himself with little to do in the first week in January. And that's when you know it's time to go back to Manhattan, or maybe Palm Beach.

Aspen socializing follows a set routine of breakfast at home or in your hotel or condo or perhaps at *Poppycocks* or sit at the share table at *Main Street Bakery and Café*. Then it's time to don your ski boots and head for the Silver Queen Gondola for the 13 minute ride to the top of Ajax Mountain. Position yourself in line next to a couple of attractive men and, voila, you will have them as your captive audience for the next quarter hour. If you somehow miscalculate and are stuck with a gondola full of girls, casually pump them for party information. You never know when you might need an extra party in a pinch.

After a run or two, ride back up and have lunch at the *Sundeck* restaurant. Try to grab a large table since everyone shares and you will want to wave over new acquaintances to join your table. Sit there long enough and you will eventually see everyone in Aspen who decided to ski Ajax that day. There is no reason to rush. A three hour lunch at the Sundeck can easily result in several party or dinner invitations and dates. The longer you sit there the more guys you will meet. Not a skier? No problem. Just buy a $20 round trip ticket on the gondola and sit at the Sundeck socializing all day long.

If you really hit the right person you may be lucky enough to be taken to the exclusive and very private *Aspen Mountain Club* next door. There you can see all of Aspen's elite at lunch in one day.

After the Sundeck closes at 3:30, ski or ride down to the bottom of the mountain and head for the *Sky Hotel* for après-ski, the Sky has a huge bar with lots of cushioned seating and is jammed to capacity by 5 p.m. in peak season. Here again you have an opportunity to meet anyone interesting that you missed or failed to talk to at lunch.

The great thing about Aspen is that you will always get another chance at that handsome guy you spotted on the chairlift. That's because you usually run into the same people two or three times every day. It's that small! If you don't see them at lunch you'll see them at après-ski or at a party or a restaurant later. They can run but they can't hide!

After collecting a few more dates and party invitations at the Sky Hotel, it's time to dress for dinner at *Matsuhisa* or *Cache Cache* or head off to a cocktail party on Red Mountain Road where the biggest houses and best parties can be found.

Wherever you end up you can be sure of one thing, the high net worth men will outnumber the women between 1.5 and 2.0 to 1.0. This contrasts with the opposite ratio of between 1.5 and 3.0 women for each man at most high-end parties in New York City. And the men will be older and wealthier than almost anywhere (except Palm Beach). The result is that once you get there, your hands need never touch your wallet since these guys will be competing to buy you drinks and dinner.

An intelligent and stylish woman can do very well in Aspen given that the competition consists largely of obvious gold diggers and overnight renters with dyed platinum hair, big surgically altered boobs and short skirts with fur boots. A little sophistication can make you stand out and take you a long way in Aspen.

The Silver Queen Gondola

As noted above, waiting in line for and riding the gondola to the top of the mountain is an unparalleled opportunity to meet high net worth men. The gondola seats six (although three of you will be facing up and three down the mountain), so wait until an auspicious looking group of guys arrives in line and jump in after them. If you change your mind, you can always let them go ahead and hang back until a man you like moves up in the line. Believe us there will be plenty of them.

By the time you get to the top you should have business cards, local phone numbers and a party invitation or two from the attractive men in your car. And if you go up around lunchtime you may get an invitation to lunch at the private *Aspen Mountain Club* restaurant. (This is where Ivana Trump and Marla Maples had their famous confrontation.)

The great news is that there is no need to ski down. Go directly to lunch at a topside restaurant then take the gondola down the mountain again. Riding the gondola/chairlifts and working the mountaintop restaurants is the most efficient ways to use the daylight hours. Ajax has the best restaurant for socializing but the restaurants on the other mountains can also provide numerous social opportunities.

The Caribou Club

The *Caribou Club*, a private membership club, is the place to be for the ambitious woman interested in high net worth nightlife. If no one you've met in line for the gondola has invited you that day, attractive women can usually talk their way in at the door. The locals have discounted memberships so your ski instructor can probably take you. Don't try going with two guys who aren't members, you won't get in. The Caribou Club gave a $1,000 per person New Year's Eve dinner in 2002. The ticket was in such demand that they ended up turning away more than 200 would-be revelers. On a normal holiday evening, the club can get so crowded you can't move, but women can do very well there because of the high ratio of high net worth men to women, so don't get discouraged. There is a back door you can sometimes sneak in but it is usually locked so don't count on it unless you have someone who can help you open it from the inside.

A beautiful woman will find it difficult to pay for anything when she goes out at night in Aspen. Usually someone will offer to buy you dinner or drinks and invite you to a party. If that doesn't happen, be sure you have made friends with the bartender to keep those free drinks coming until someone interesting does come along. If you look good and smile, we guarantee someone will.

The Party Situation

The New Year's parties on Red Mountain Road are a sight to behold. If you have networked effectively over the prior two or three days, you should have a few invitations to choose from. Many Aspen families give a party every year on the same day. They try to stagger the days between Christmas and New Year's so that there is a major party to go to every night until January 1st. After January 1st, the parties drop off abruptly so make sure you get to Aspen by December 26th in order not to miss the big events.

The Competition

The competition is intense but there are enough high net worth men around so that you will have plenty of opportunities. In fact high net worth men greatly outnumber the women in Aspen. As in most very high-end resorts, you will find professional competition here. The LA media moguls seem to have a particular penchant for flying in hookers from Las Vegas. But don't get discouraged. The wealthy man you see with a hooker on a Tuesday night will likely be free again on Wednesday morning.

CHAPTER SEVENTEEN

ST. TROPEZ –
CÔTE D'AZUR

The Gold Digging Capital of the Côte d'Azur in the South of France is a little fishing village called St. Tropez. Here rapacious European playboys mingle with young models and the Hollywood fast crowd to create a frenetic drug and alcohol fueled moneyfest for the super rich. You will also encounter numerous financially pressed toxic European males who may be single, divorced or married–although you may never find out which.

The French, English and Italian playboys here are dangerous, predatory and extremely charming. They possess a level of weathered worldliness that you will not find in the U.S. You may find yourself unprepared for the level of treachery and deceit these guys can reach. There are numerous stories of young girls being lured to a "modeling job" and ending up drugged and raped in one of the big chateaux in the hills above the village.

Nevertheless, a smart girl can be safely swept into a whirlwind of non-stop party action. Dinner starts after 10 P.M. At 1:00 A.M. head to *Les Caves du Roy* in the *Hotel Byblos* where you can party till dawn. The hotel is a great place to stay if you can find someone to share the $1,000 plus per night room rate. The last time we were there Bruce Willis was staying in the next room and Elizabeth Hurley was also staying in the hotel. If you can afford the $50 cheeseburger go there for lunch.

When you wake up at 2 P.M., don't worry, it's still not too late to head for the beach. Cab it to *Club 55* (*Cinquante-Cinq*) just a few miles out of town. Parking can be very tight and a towel and mat can be had there for just over $100 for the day. But if you are feeling too frugal to lease a towel, just sit in the beach restaurants with a girlfriend. Within five minutes you will be invited to a table filled with attractive bronzed Europeans. You can sit there all day socializing, eating and drinking with your new friends who are unlikely to ask for more than a token contribution to the check. They will likely invite you to a glamorous dinner party that night in the hills and you will be all set for the rest of your stay. Don't worry about having no time to swim. No one goes in the water. Lying topless in the sand (or on a towel) or sitting in the restaurant is the order of the day here.

In the early evening sit at a café in the port or walk along the harbor past the rows of big yachts. A quick stroll can result in invitations to dinner, a party and maybe a night or two on board a major yacht. To get oriented sit in the port and pick out the boat or boats you want to be on. If you're looking good, an invitation may be the immediate result.

Once you've caught your European millionaire of choice, make him take you for a romantic stay at the *Hotel du Cap* in Cap d'Antibes or perhaps the *Colombe d'Or* in St. Paul-de-Vence.

Hotel du Cap-Eden-Roc is one of the most spectacular hotels in the world and among the most expensive. Amazingly, they don't take credit cards. It's cash only at the Hotel du Cap and they know how to extract it with a vengeance. A decent room will run you $1,000 per night, a really nice one $1,500. Drinks range from $30-$50 depending on the staff's mood and towels at the pool will set you back another $75 per couple. There is almost nothing you can have that they don't charge you extra for and, of course, the staff expects big tips on top of the extortionate prices. Both the lobby and the visually spectacular swimming area (which includes a diving board and climbing ropes into the sea near a dangerous cliff) are blanketed with video surveillance, perhaps to stop your beau from walking out without paying for your towels.

If you get bored at the Hotel du Cap–there is nothing to do at the hotel except sit at the pool with your man watching him hemorrhage money–convince him to move you to the Colombe d'Or. Located in the unbelievably picturesque hilltop fortified castle of St. Paul-de-Vence, the Colombe d'Or is both a beautiful hotel and one of the world's best restaurants.

You can have a spectacular meal, and after dinner stroll through the winding village streets and get your guy to bed for an all night love fest with little competition in sight. But reserve as soon as you find your guy. The Colombe d'Or is booked up months in advance. If you can't get in, the *Hotel St. Paul* makes a good second choice for your romantic getaway. If you don't get along with your guy in these romantic spots you won't get along with him anywhere. In that case go back to St. Tropez and find another one!

It won't take long.

CHAPTER EIGHTEEN

OFF CIRCUIT GOLD DIGGING

Gold is everywhere. Any place that wealthy men walk, sit or stand is a place that you can do business. You never know when that golden opportunity may arise so you should always look your best. The one time you leave the house looking like a charwoman from *Oliver Twist*, may be the time that Ted Turner walks by your front door.

Manhattan, Southampton, St. Tropez, St. Barths, Palm Beach and Aspen are great major league Gold Digging destinations. But you can pan for gold at home in your own community. However, you will have to be much more focused on specific individuals than on the High Net Worth Dating Circuit. If you are lying on the beach in Southampton in front of the Southampton Bathing Corporation (having strolled down from the public beach where you parked your car), you may have 30-40 multi-millionaires scan your lithe bikini clad body in the space of an hour or two.

To meet one all you have to do is stand up and smile at him or join his volleyball or Frisbee game.

On the other hand if you live in a small town in Illinois, Texas or Louisiana, this just isn't going to happen. Instead you will have to investigate and target the specific high net worth individuals who live in your area. Find out what clubs your target belongs to and what restaurants he favors for lunch and dinner. Look into which upscale charities hold benefits in your area. Get on a committee. Find out who the most desirable party guests in your area are. You will find that tracking down and meeting your target will involve a fair amount of work. You may succeed in meeting him only to find that he is in a committed relationship or isn't interested in you. So always work on three or four targets at a time and be prepared for rejection. Of course, if you live in a very small town you will already know everything you need to know about your fellow residents. The difficulty will be in operating without attracting so much comment that your good work is sabotaged by nosey girlfriends and competitors.

Using the techniques in this book, a determined woman can track, meet and marry a rich man almost anywhere that there are wealthy men to track. But the odds are greatly improved if you stalk your prey on the established high net worth circuit. Finding a wealthy man is in part a numbers game. And the big numbers will be found at the regular stops on the major league benefit and social circuit.

CHAPTER NINETEEN

THE FORTUNE 60 – THE RICHEST SINGLE OR DIVORCED MEN IN AMERICA

Think there are no single super rich left for you? Think again.
Here's a list of 60 single or divorced guys who made the recent
Forbes or *Fortune 400* list of the wealthiest men in America.

Name	Wealth	Age	Marital Status
Paul Allen	$22.0 billion	50	Single
Lawrence J. Ellison	$18.0 billion	59	Divorced
Ty Warner	$6.0 billion	59	Single
Kirk Kerkorian	$5.0 billion	86	Divorced
Michael Bloomberg	$4.9 billion	61	Divorced
John Menard, Jr.	$3.5 billion	63	Divorced
George Lucas	$3.0 billion	59	Divorced

George Kaiser	$3.0 billion	61	Widowed
Donald Trump	$2.5 billion	57	Divorced
Ted Turner	$2.3 billion	64	Divorced
Charles Butt	$2.3 billion	65	Single
Herb Allen	$1.8 billion	63	Divorced
Edward Gaybird	$1.8 billion	84	Widowed
B. Wayne Hughes	$1.8 billion	70	Divorced
Bruce Kovner	$1.8 billion	58	Divorced
Steven Rales	$1.7 billion	46	Divorced
Alec Gores	$1.6 billion	50	Divorced
David Filo	$1.6 billion	37	Single
B. Thomas Golisano	$1.6 billion	61	Divorced
Laurence Rockefeller	$1.5 billion	93	Widowed*
Fayez Sarofim	$1.5 billion	74	Divorced
Jackson Stephens	$1.5 billion	80	Divorced
John Sperling	$1.5 billion	82	Divorced
Jon L. Stryker	$1.5 billion	45	Single
Bruce Duner	$1.4 billion	58	Divorced
Robert Naify	$1.4 billion	81	Widowed
Mark Cuban	$1.3 billion	44	Single
Robert Johnson	$1.3 billion	57	Divorced
Peter Lewis	$1.3 billion	69	Divorced
Ted Field	$1.2 billion	51	Divorced
Daniel Ziff	$1.2 billion	31	Single
David Hearst, Jr.	$1.2 billion	58	Single
Albert Lee Ueltschi	$1.2 billion	86	Widowed
Mort Zuckerman	$1.2 billion	66	Divorced
Austin Hearst	$1.2 billion	51	Divorced
John Arillaga	$1.1 billion	66	Widowed
O. Bruton Smith	$1.1 billion	76	Divorced
Charles Simonyi	$1.0 billion	55	Single
Roger Milliken	$1.0 billion	87	Widowed
Neil Bluhm	$1.0 billion	65	Divorced
Alfred Mann	$1.0 billion	77	Divorced
Thomas Bailey	$975 million	66	Divorced
Dwight Opperman	$975 million	80	Widowed
Edmund Ansin	$950 million	67	Divorced
William Levine	$940 million	71	Widowed

Ernest Gallo	$930 million	94	Widowed
Marvin Oates	$825 million	80	Divorced
Leonardo Rizzuto	$770 million	65	Divorced
Alberto Vilar	$750 million	62	Divorced
Walter Shorenstein	$750 million	88	Widowed
Todd Wagner	$750 million	43	Single
Philip Ruffin	$750 million	67	Divorced
Teddy Forstman	$725 million	63	Single
Norman Wait, Jr.	$700 million	49	Divorced
Frederich Koch	$650 million	67	Single
William Koch	$650 million	63	Divorced
Tom Werner	$600 million	53	Single
Sydell Miller	$595 million	65	Widowed
Sergey Brin	$550 million	30	Single
Larry Page	$550 million	30	Single

There–now you have some obvious targets. Get to work and go for one of them! And do it quickly, before they die single! What a waste that would be!

* Sorry, you're too late. He died in October 2004.

PART FOUR

High Net Worth Dating Strategies

CHAPTER TWENTY

DITCH THE NOT RICH

You may attend several charity benefits each month, but you are not running a charity. High-end Gold Diggers do not waste time on men with a net worth of less than US$10.0 million and annual income of less than US$1,000,000. This is the Minimum Net Wealth Standard ("MNWS").

If your boyfriend is a starving artist in Manhattan's East Village and his bathtub and toilet are in the living room, you will need to change boyfriends. High-end Gold Diggers do not date the poor. We are already poor. Been there, done that.

There are a number of other circumstances that will require you to drop your boyfriend.

13 Reasons to Change Boyfriends

You must change boyfriends when:

(1) You discover he fails to meet the Minimum Net Wealth Standard for any year in the past three years.

(2) There is no lock on his bathroom door.

(3) He harangues you for not eating enough.

(4) He catches you purging or putting food in your purse.

(5) He is cheap (i.e., he fails to pay for anything you demand or fails to give you lots of nice restaurant meals).

(6) You have not received a piece of jewelry with a retail value of at least $5,000 and you have been dating for six months.

(7) You have not received an engagement ring and you have been dating for 13 months or more.

(8) He is not single or his divorce decree has not been legally effective for at least 18 months.

(9) He lives with his mother.

(10) He lives outside of Manhattan, does not own his Manhattan apartment or lives above 96th Street.

(11) He does not own a house in either Palm Beach, Aspen, the Hamptons, Martha's Vineyard or Nantucket.

(12) Your background check reveals him to be a womanizer.

(13) He does not want to have children, repeatedly speaks disparagingly of marriage, has dated more than 15 women in the last 12 months, or is not sexually attracted to you in a big way.

If your boyfriend has any of these unlucky 13 characteristics, dump him without delay.

Why?

Because he is never going to marry you. That's why. And he is not going to spend enough money on you to make being with him worth your while.

Characteristics You Should Look for in a Boyfriend

A proper boyfriend should be:

(1) Old enough to be your father.

(2) Rich enough to meet the Minimum Net Wealth Standard.

(3) Insecure enough to try to impress you with his riches. If he flies you to Palm Beach in his private jet, charters a plane for you or buys you major jewelry in the first days or weeks after meeting you, you are in business.

(4) Without easy access to models.

(5) Butt-ugly or at least not especially good-looking.

(6) Willing to let you redecorate.

(7) Without children at home.

(8) Willing to do what you tell him to do.

(9) Less manipulative than you are, and the more easygoing the better.

(10) Blissfully unaware of the extent of your gold digging agenda, your eating disorder, your psychotic or neurotic tendencies, medical regimens, massive insecurities, multiple bipolar personalities and recurrent yeast infections.

Chapter twenty-one

QUIT YOUR DAY JOB

O n the High Net Worth Dating Circuit there are two things High-end Gold Diggers don't do much of.

(1) We don't eat much.

(2) We don't work much.

You Probably Don't Have Time to Work

A successful Gold Digger doesn't have time for a job. As an ambitious woman you have too many other things to do. Here's how a High-end Gold Digger spends her time:

(1) Not eating in restaurants.

(2) Working out.

(3) Spa treatments to relax from working out and not working.

(4) Sleeping 10-12 hours a day to keep yourself in a tip-top state of restfulness (Note: If you are taking lots of amphetamines, you can reduce your sleeping time drastically to have more time for the other listed activities).

(5) Shopping so you are always dressed to perfection.

(6) Party planning with your friends. Planning the parties you give and the ones you attend in detail.

(7) Attending charity events, parties, dinner parties, cocktail parties, benefit parties, weddings, media events, trendy night-clubs, bars & restaurants and business conferences.

(8) Taking intensive classes in gardening, decorating and tantric sex.

(9) Getting your hair done, catalogue studying, web surfing and looking in the mirror.

(10) Driving your men crazy with desire, and breaking them down psychologically, mentally and physically until they give you a big engagement ring.

It is simply impossible to work full-time and focus on these 10 important tasks with the intensity necessary to achieve your goal and lasso your targeted fiancé. While occasional modeling is okay, a full-time job will take you out of the Gold Digger's mindset and drain the energy you need to stay thin and land that wealthy husband.

As women we have limited time. Given our nearly starved condition, we have even more limited energy. We need to use it to get our guy. Don't try to be a superwoman. Working full-time while you are starving to death is not a realistic option.

Of course, there are some jobs you can have; provided they aren't too taxing. Here are 13 lucky ones.

The 13 Best Jobs

(1) Selling high-end residential real estate;

(2) Selling G-5's or other private jets;

(3) Receptionist at Chelsea or 57th Street art gallery;

(4) Working at Sotheby's or Christie's;

(5) Being a publicist or event planner;

(6) Modeling;

(7) Being a non-working actress;

(8) Flight Attendant (particularly for Hooter-Air);

(9) Anything you can do from home (e.g., freelance writer);

(10) Socialite;

(11) Part-time work for non-profit organizations;

(12) Any job at Condé Nast; or

(13) Aspen ski instructor.

While some women have struck gold while working as waitresses, call girls or escorts, these are very much hit or miss occupations. It all depends on the clientele you get. And the clientele can be quite unpredictable. Selling or chartering private jets or high-end real estate on the other hand is a no lose proposition.

We can't name names, but we understand that a number of real estate brokers at Sotheby's International Realty have had affairs with and occasionally landed a number of high net worth apartment buyers. While some cynical types might suggest that these brokers' favors are included in the brokerage fee, we view it differently. These women are just seeking the more secure position of a high net worth wife. And who can blame them for wanting to live in the palatial apartments they sell at Sotheby's. One was even heard to sniff to a colleague about a perfectly nice young investment banker, that she couldn't date anyone if they were buying an apartment for a mere $1.6 million. Her beau would have to be in the $2.5 million and up range.

Now that's a girl with her eye on the ball!

CHAPTER TWENTY-TWO

CAMPAIGN STRATEGY – RAISING YOUR PROFILE

The quest for a high net worth husband must be planned with the seriousness of any major military or political campaign. High net worth dating is the moral equivalent of war.

You must outsmart and out-smile the competition at every turn. You must be focused. You must be aware.

Here are three over-the-top ways to raise your profile among high net worth males:

Hire a Publicist

A girl in the news gets attention. Being written up in magazines and gossip columns will automatically make you more desirable.

Men love boasting about how accomplished and desirable their girlfriend or wife is. Having a woman in the news is an ego trip for any guy. The higher your profile the more men you will attract.

You will also attract more successful men if you have a media profile. Successful and celebrity men like to date celebrity women because it helps their image. Many successful men will only seriously date high profile women.

There is nothing shameful about hiring a publicist. All the best people have one.

We know one mid 30s lass who was not satisfied with the quality of the dates she was getting. While her family owned a large New York media company, she was not particularly high profile. The publicist got her glowing articles in *Time* magazine and New York magazine. Both ran flattering pictures. Her dating life immediately picked up. Within a week after these articles appeared she was dating the CEO of a Fortune 500 company.

It is almost impossible for publicity to be negative. Sure you don't want to be written up for shoplifting, crashing your car into loads of strangers or giving the President a blow job, but short of that almost any publicity is good publicity.

Get in the Society Pages

One way to start getting coverage is by getting invited to and crashing lots of parties. Befriend the people you see being photographed at parties. Stand next to them when pictures are being taken. Chat up the society photographers like New York City's Patrick McMullan and his assistants. You will see the same photographers at every party. Once one magazine starts taking pictures of you, they all will.

Date a Celebrity

Dating a celebrity can give an enormous boost to your social career. Celebrity males go through so many women that you have as good a shot as anyone. Make a play for one by standing next to him. Once you have dated a celebrity, no one can take that away from you.

Your future dating prospects will increase. People will whisper that you went out with Keith Hernandez or Roger Clemens, Jay McInerney, Mick Jagger, Chappy Morris, Mario Lemieux, Donald Trump, Ron Perelman, Warren Beatty, Puffy Combs or Jack Nicholson.

Yeah. And who hasn't?

It doesn't matter. Having dated a celebrity will give you instant credibility at any cocktail party. At least until your celebrity's star starts to fade. One date is sufficient. A one-night stand is perfect. You can milk a one-night stand with Jack Nicholson or Warren Beatty for years. And practically all you have to do to get a celebrity into bed is to stand next him.

The celebrity will do the rest.

CHAPTER TWENTY-THREE

DATING TIPS – THE BASICS

The First Date

T he first date is basically a reconnaissance operation. You are doing preliminary due diligence and confirming the prior intelligence you have gathered. The goal of the first date is to get the following information and a second date:

(1) His real estate holdings.

(2) His divorces, marriages (previous owners), children (competing heirs) and other long-term relationships.

(3) Where he summers.

(4) What he does (if anything).

(5) Family, money or self-made? If family money, who controls the purse strings?

(6) How rich is he?

Encourage him to talk about his interests and possessions. Listen to him. Look him in the eye. Find out if he is happy. Indicate you share an interest in anything he likes or owns. Make him begin to suspect that you are his soul mate. Sit there and look gorgeous. Talk as little as possible. Make him work to impress you.

At the end of the evening, give him a good night kiss that hints at something more. Do not betray excessive interest. Save the tongue for later.

The Second Date

If all went well, he will soon call you for another dinner. You don't need to call him.

Second dates can sometimes be flat. The excitement of the first get together is over and you both know you are not likely to have sex that night. Use the second date to fill in the gaps in your knowledge of his background. Talk to him about things he likes to do. Your job is to keep him interested and get to that all important Third Date.

He may ask you back to his house or apartment for a drink. If you are still interested in him you can go, but make it very clear that you can only stay for a short time. Make him give you a complete tour of the house. Look at every room. Every furnishing and knick-knack is an indicator of his wealth or lack of it. Take the opportunity to use the bathroom. Check all cabinets for evidence of female presence. Look for antidepressants and other prescription drugs. You want to know what you are dealing with.

Usually he will make you a drink and ask you to sit next to him on the couch. He will try to kiss you. Go with it for a few minutes. When he starts to unhook your bra, it's time to go. The more breathless you leave him the faster he will call you for date number three.

The Third Date and Beyond – Don't Go to Bed Without Your Dinner

Congratulations! You made it to the third date.
Now you can fool around. But keep in mind that it is unhealthy to have sex on an empty stomach. If you don't get a good meal before you sleep with him you won't get one afterwards. At best it will be Chinese take-out food.

Some guys will try anything to get you into bed without buying you dinner. They will suggest meeting for drinks after dinner, they will propose going to a late movie, they will want to meet up at 11:00 p.m. to go clubbing. These guys want to sleep with you for the price of two or three drinks.

Make it clear that this is not going to work.

There is no point in going on a drinks date. You won't have time to get to know him and you'll end up having to cook yourself a meal when you get home at one o'clock in the morning. And most likely your dream guy will turn out to be a Humper and Dumper.

Humping and Dumping

Some guys like to hump and dump. It's not personal. It's just what they do. There is nothing in it for you to date a man like this. His definition of "eternity" is the time between his coming and your going. He won't even want you spending the night at his house after you have had sex. He will want you out before *Letterman* comes on.

Don't let one of these guys do the hump and dump with you!

CHAPTER TWENTY-FOUR

MARKING YOUR TERRITORY – LEAVING THINGS AT HIS HOUSE

Put Your Panties and Earrings to Work

High net worth dating is the moral equivalent of war. And it is a fight to the finish. You have to battle for your man with every available weapon. Now that you are past the third date, one of the most important guerilla warfare tactics you can use is to leave your panties or earrings at his house. A bracelet or bra or almost any other article of clothing can be extremely effective in smoking out and ridding yourself of unwanted rivals, wives and other pests.

Always carry an extra pair of inexpensive but sexy panties and earrings to use for this purpose. Push the extra panties between the mattress and headboard or hide them at the foot of the bed between the bottom sheet and the edge of the mattress. Leave one earring on the floor beside the bed on your side so he won't notice it. Put the other one in the bathroom behind the toilet. Then place lipstick or your cologne in his bathroom cabinet and hide a love note in his mail.

Men rarely notice these things right away. Often they don't clean their own apartment so these objects are likely to stay right where they are until the cleaning lady comes or another woman finds them. If he is dating someone else, she will definitely find whatever you leave behind. She may even suspect that he is seeing more than one other woman. This should provoke a huge fight. With any luck your unseen rival(s) will storm out never to return after catching him red-handed with your panties in his bed.

If you didn't bring extra earrings and don't want to leave the good ones you are wearing, stuff the used condom wrapper between the sheets. This can be just as effective.

Some very sophisticated men are onto this trick. They carefully search the entire apartment until they find whatever you have left.

One wicked Wall Streeter actually has a shoebox on his dresser where he keeps earrings, panties and bracelets. The sign on it reads,

"Not responsible for objects left more than 30 days."

"They take it with them or claim it quickly, or they lose it," he says with a grin.

Fortunately, most guys are not that smart.

Leaving your stuff at his house is one aspect of the larger subject of psychological warfare which we will address in Chapter 27 – "The Golden Hooks."

CHAPTER TWENTY-FIVE

HIGH MAINTENANCE – TO BE OR NOT TO BE, THAT IS THE QUESTION

We know a glamorous thirty-something socialite–let's call her Emily–who seems to have it all but somehow can't keep a guy. Emily does everything by the book. She insists that the dates pick her up at her apartment building and take her home at the end of the evening. She never reaches into her wallet (we wonder if she even owns one), won't walk to any destination more than two blocks away and is most comfortable drinking champagne while surrounded by a group of single men. Emily is impeccably dressed, well-mannered, perfectly coiffed and owns all the right handbags. She won't fly to Aspen for the weekend unless her date springs for a first class ticket. Most of New York's high profile men have been on at least one date with her. Yet she never seems to have a relationship that lasts more than six months. A wealthy bachelor she had hopes of marrying was quoted in the press reffering to her as "reliable arm candy."

What is Emily doing wrong?

The answer is she is doing everything wrong. She is aggravating her dates. She is focusing only on herself not on making her dates feel comfortable. Some men may not like having to pick her up and drop her off at her door. Others may object that she never contributes a penny to their time together. Others may not like the way she flirts at parties. And some men may not appreciate being snarled at when they forget to hold the door for Emily or allow her into the taxi first. Others resent her rule on not having sex until the tenth date. Still others resent buying her first class plane tickets.

It is true that most men like to do things for a woman. They like to make an effort to please her. But in Emily's case men feel daunted. There is no payoff. Her demands are endless. Her men can't imagine how they are ever going to keep her happy. And if a man does not think he has the ability to make you happy he will dump you. Men know instinctively if a woman is too difficult for them to please. And Emily is just too difficult to please.

Emily has a bad case of High Maintenance. She thinks she is just weeding out men who won't treasure her the way she wants to be treasured. In fact, she is repelling every man she meets.

The only type of man who will go for Emily is one who is very insecure or submissive. A man who likes being pushed around. Emily does not like men like this. She is not a dominatrix. She just wants a man who will treat her like a princess.

But Emily won't be attracting any princes. In fact, she will be lucky to get a frog.

The important point here is to do some self-examination. How are your behaviors and routines filtering the men you meet or want to meet? Are you repelling the very types you want to attract?

If you want to meet a quiet, wealthy businessman and move to the suburbs, think about the social activities you engage in. Are you going to loads of fashion and media events and not meeting any appropriate guys? Do you work for a fashion house where all the men around you are gay? If so, you are not likely to meet your guy. Quiet, family oriented, high net worth men do not attend fashion and media events. Those functions are attended by trendy and sometimes toxic bachelors and young and wild investment bankers. Consider doing more socializing at private clubs like New York City's Doubles, Soho House, the Downtown Association or the Yale Club. Avoid parties populated by models and fashionistas. Your behavior, activities, appearance and social schedule must be focused on the type of guy you want. Otherwise the various pieces of your life will work at cross purposes.

If you want a Jewish man or a Catholic guy, attend events where Jewish men or Catholic guys go. Don't go to the "all WASP all the time" parties at the Museum of the City of New York or the Frick. If you want a sports star, hang out where the sports stars go. Don't go to the Museum of Natural History's annual charity ball.

CHAPTER TWENTY-SIX

DON'T DEMAND YOUR DUE
TOO SOON

Never Start by Asking for Money from Your Target

You are not a mistress or a hooker. You are not focused on short-term income. You are going for the big pot of gold at the end of that long planned honeymoon. You should be careful about requesting or accepting cash gifts from your man until after you are engaged to be married.

Of course, if he wants to buy you a sexy dress, a necklace, bracelet or watch that is fine, as long as it is a gift from him and not a demand from you.

Asking for money will instantly change the nature and quality of your relationship. He may see you in a new and negative light. He may lose trust in you. He may begin to suspect your real motives and background.

Forming a bond with a man is about getting him to trust you. He is not going to trust you if you walk in asking for money. Trust means that he believes you have his best interests at heart, not your own. Show him he can trust you by turning down offers of cash and overly extravagant gifts. First you have to cement a relationship. The cash and overly extravagant gifts will come later.

Many newly wealthy men like to show off by spending money in extravagant ways. One bachelor we know likes to send a private plane to pick up a girl he has invited for the weekend to his North Carolina retreat. He may give her an expensive watch or bracelet on the second date.

This kind of behavior shows genuine insecurity and a certain amount of lack of respect for you. He is communicating that he thinks you can be bought. Of course he is right. But you can't let him know this. Painful as it may be to do so, turn down the lavish gifts. Tell him you are impressed by a strong man or a loving man, not by money. Tell him you appreciate his thoughtfulness but it is too soon to accept gifts from him. Make it clear that he has to win you over based on his human qualities first. This will get his attention.

Remember that he is displaying his wealth and giving you the watch for his own reasons. He wants to get you to sleep with him sooner than you otherwise would. This may not be in your long-term interest. Take your time and do your research. You may find that he ships in several girls a week for casual sex. This is not your kind of guy. A guy like that is unlikely to value one woman enough to spend his life with her. And from his toxic bachelor's perspective why should he? He can always fly in a new planeload of girls for cheap sex and companionship if any of the old ones prove annoying or tiresome.

The Mistress Apartment

As your relationship develops over time, you may want him to get you a new apartment that he is responsible for. Ideally, he should buy it for you. If he rents it he can always stop making the payments and you will be out on the street with nothing to show for it. Hotel heir John Tisch was reported by the press to have stopped paying the rent on an apartment in a Tisch family owned building which had been leased to his long time, young girlfriend after she gave him the Ultimatum during a trip to the Caribbean. The poor girl, who had been living a life of luxury, overplayed her hand and was forced to move back with her family in Texas.

There are risks to accepting a rented apartment from your target. You will lose leverage over him if you do. It is safer to keep your apartment or house unless he is willing to buy you a new place outright.

The Dreaded Co-op Board

Strict board approval requirements make it difficult for high net worth men to purchase or even rent cooperative apartments in Manhattan for their mistresses and lovers. Condominiums, however, present no such obstacles for either renters or purchasers. But condominiums are relatively rare on Manhattan's desirable upper East Side.

Fortunately, Donald Trump has provided the perfect solution on Central Park South – the Mistress Building. Located on the Southside of 59th Street near Sixth Avenue, the apartment complex is known in the real estate trade as the Mistress Building because of the numerous single women residing there in apartments purchased or rented for them by married men.

CHAPTER TWENTY-SEVEN

THE GOLDEN HOOKS

A man will not marry you unless he feels he has to. It's up to you to make sure he gives you the ring. Here are some deal closing tips from the experts on giving him compelling reasons to ask you to marry him.

Creating a Triangle

The most effective way to get a man to give you a ring is to make him feel he is about to lose you to another guy. To execute this simple strategy, you need an additional suitor. Let's call him Bob. Your target, Chapwick, has been giving you problems lately. Whenever you bring up the subject of children or marriage or point out how happy a couple you are, Chapwick goes silent. His eyes glaze over. He tries to change the subject. He is spending one or two weekends a month traveling without you. Or maybe you and Chapwick are already living together but he won't commit.

Fortunately, a solution is at hand. Namely, Bob. Not that you would ever consider marrying Bob. But Chapwick might think you would.

When Chappy next calls for a date, thank him but tell him you have a dinner engagement - but don't say with whom. When he asks say, "Bob. I think you know him, don't you? I think Bob is so much fun." This will get his attention. Chapwick will start calling you at 10 p.m. to see if you are home from dinner. You know you've got him worried.

Have a few more dates with Bob. They can be real dates or pretend ones where you actually are out with your girlfriends.

Eventually Chappy will want to have a talk with you about Bob.

When he tells you to stop seeing Bob, give it to him straight.

"Chappy, I love you so much and I've always thought of us as being together. But I just can't wait any longer for a decision. I want you to make up your mind about our future. Unless you do this by _____ [here fill in a specific deadline, not more than three months away] I've decided I'm going to pursue other options."

Then finish with a flourish.

"I love you dearly, but I can't wait forever for you to make up that stubborn male mind of yours. I want us to get started on building a great life together."

If nothing happens, you have been too subtle. When the deadline passes, call him and explain clearly why you are dumping him. Then refuse to see him when he calls.

If he really wants you, he will chase after you with a ring. If he doesn't react, it means he would have never married you anyway and you've just smoked him out. Either way you have lost nothing. You've either gained a husband or you have saved yourself lots of time and heartache.

The Ultimatum

The Ultimatum is your line in the sand. It is the time you announce by which you must be officially and publicly engaged or you will have to dump him. When you give him the Ultimatum you have to mean it. The Ultimatum is best given when you have created a triangle. He will feel much more pressure if he knows you have an alternative lined up. But used forcefully, the Ultimatum alone can provide the necessary force to move him off the dime.

Make it clear from the beginning that you don't date casually. You are not a party girl. He should understand that you want a serious commitment and not a casual fling. And don't let him put you off when you decide it's time to discuss your future.

At the same time, whining and nagging will get you nowhere. If he feels pressured and anxious it is always easier for him to rationalize dumping you rather than marrying you.

Many women have lost their guys by bringing up the Ultimatum too soon or with the wrong tone. You must be firm yet loving. And don't let him change the subject.

Tell him you want to start a family. Tell him you can't risk being with someone who is not serious about you. Explain that you have other options. And give him a definite and unambiguous timetable for making his decision. Then shut up about it for awhile. Let the impact sink in for a few weeks. Use this time to be as loving and positive as you can be.

When you have him in a soft and loving mood, say lying in bed after sex, you should bring it up gently. "Have you thought any more about our conversation?"

His reaction will tell you what you need to know. If he says he isn't ready to commit, believe him. He means it. Cut your losses and move on.

Many women don't understand that when faced with the Ultimatum, a man who says he isn't ready really means it. He isn't going to marry you. Don't delude yourself in thinking otherwise. It was tough for him to say that. He would have much preferred to lie. So when he says he isn't   interested in marriage you'd better believe he is telling the truth.

More often men will play for time. One ingenious bachelor we know told his girl that he would make a decision in six months but that "every time she mentioned the subject of marriage the decision point would automatically get extended for another two weeks." He got away with this for three years!

CHAPTER TWENTY-EIGHT

ASK NOT WHAT YOUR INTENDED CAN DO FOR YOU – ASK WHAT YOU CAN DO FOR YOUR INTENDED

Your target is not going to ask you to marry him just because you want him to. He isn't going to marry you because you need to be married. He is only going to marry you if he has strong and compelling reasons why he should. If you want him, you have to show him why it is in his best interest to marry you.

Be an Asset

Many women make the mistake of focusing far too much on themselves and what they want. Believe us when we tell you that your target does not care what you want at all. In fact, it is fair to say that nothing could be further from his mind.

He will only be interested in doing what he wants to do and what it is in his best interest to do. Your job is to prove to him beyond any reasonable doubt that marrying you is in his best interest.

Your wealthy intended is your judge, jury and potentially your executioner. He can dump you any time he decides that you no longer fit into his plans or that it is in his best interests to do so. He may dump you for these reasons even if he is enormously attracted to you. So make sure you focus on the right thing. Concentrate on being an asset to him. Focus on what he needs and wants not what you want.

Know Your Man's Needs, Skills and Goals

As you continue dating you should be developing a comprehensive psychological profile of your target. Use this profile to come up with ways to add value to his life. This is the only way to get him to add value to yours.

His psychological profile should cover at least the following subjects:

What Are His Interests?

Find out what really gets him excited. If he is a dedicated collector of pre-Colombian sculpture or a fanatic about wine or Roman law, or even if he is addicted to watching football on TV or playing golf on weekends, learn something about his favorite subjects. Do research on-line or spend a couple of days in the public library. Then surprise him with a conversational tidbit that shows your knowledge of the subject. It may make him look at you in a whole new light.

If he starts talking about his fascination with Jackson Pollock, tell him that Lee Krasner, Pollock's wife is believed to have passed off several of her own works as Pollock's in an effort to build up her own reputation. He will be most impressed if what you say is plausible but little known to the public or something that is only suspected by real experts.

Your guy already thinks somewhat highly of you. After all he is dating you. And he is probably desperately hoping that you are his soul mate. Showing knowledge of the things he is most interested in will make you all the more fascinating to him.

His Weaknesses Are Your Opportunities

Nobody is Superman. Nobody can do it all. Identifying his weaknesses can be very important in making yourself seem a complimentary partner. If he lacks social skills you can be the gracious partner who makes his social and business interactions go more smoothly. If he is hopeless at decorating his homes, you can step in and make this your project. If he needs someone to smooth over relations with his wealthy parents who control the purse strings, you can be the bridge to a new relationship with his parents. If he is a slob, you can help him by picking up after him. If he eats poorly or can't cook, you can make him healthy and regular meals at home. At his house you can bond much more completely than you would through a succession of restaurant meals. You should see how every flaw he has is a further opportunity to bond with him.

All this may seem like work. And you don't want to be his maid or appointments secretary. But don't miss the point. All these tasks are opportunities for you to add value by being helpful. This is work that will get you into the fabric of his life. This is work that can pay off big.

We know one lovely lass who landed a very wealthy New York doctor and avid car collector in part by using this simple technique of being helpful. She moved into his Palm Beach residence, and took over administration of the house to the point of washing all of his cars by hand herself every time he flew down from New York.

Her devotion paid off and she is now married with a child by her new husband and is leading a life of luxury on the New York, Palm Beach and Southampton social circuit.

What Are His Skills and Abilities?

Is he athletic? Does he ski, water ski or play polo? Is he good at math, tennis or Ping Pong? Does he write well? Is he a good public speaker? Can he cook? Does he box or do karate? Does he have a sense of humor? Does he like children? Can he take care of an animal? Is he social? How's his gardening? Is he a good lover? Does he eat well? Dress well? Look well? Does he have a good eye for art? If he loves tennis and plays it well, take some lessons. If he dresses poorly help him look better. Look for any way that you can complement his skill or lack of skill in specific areas. This will help you integrate your life with his. This kind of integration is a prerequisite for the bonding that is essential in a permanent relationship.

CHAPTER TWENTY-NINE

TAKING OVER

Change His Life

The fastest and surest way to cement your bond with your high net worth prospect is to take over as many aspects of his life as you can manage.

Start by arranging his social life. After all why should he have a social life without you? You decide who he should see and where you both should go in the evening. Eliminate all activities with undesirable friends and colleagues. Steer him away from model parties and media events. Go wherever he goes. "Often a woman is the one who organizes a couple's social life," says one prominent socialite who is married to a billionaire industrialist. "The man who is working hard does not have time to pay attention to that."

Focus on his house or apartment and how he lives his daily routine. Redo or clean out his closets. Start decorating. Throw out or hide his clothes that you dislike. Rearrange the furniture in his living room

Express interest in everything he does and in improving the organization of every part of his life. Insinuate yourself into every aspect of his day. You will find that you can gradually take control of his life and move it in the direction you want.

Hire His Coach or Shrink

Find a shrink or life coach that you trust and who believes in marriage and relationships. Offer to hire him the coach or shrink as a way of solving some problem he is having in his business or personal life. If you must pay this person with your own money to steer your man in the direction you want. Some women have had great success in getting a life coach who pushed their target into thinking in a more responsible and long-term fashion about his relationships. Having a coach in his life to whom you can feed suggestions which will be passed on as objective professional advice can be a very effective technique.

In due course, you will be planning his social calendar, deciding where to go on vacation, redoing his home, re-landscaping his garden and organizing and co-hosting his parties.

At first he may be bemused by your enthusiastic efforts to reorganize his life. But as you gradually assume control of his day-to-day activities, you will begin to feel his resistance to you breaking down. By taking over, you are convincing him that you care about him deeply. And that is what he wants to think his future wife would do.

There simply is no better way to establish yourself as a permanent fixture in his life than to get control of his daily routine.

CHAPTER THIRTY

10 WAYS TO MAKE HIM BOND WITH YOU

Bonding 101

It isn't easy to make a busy high net worth mogul bond with you emotionally. In fact, it may appear that your target has no emotions. Don't worry, you can bond with even the most narcissistic man by using the following ten techniques. These techniques have one thing in common. They are all about doing things for him, making him happy, showing how much you adore him and how willing you are to change anything about yourself that he doesn't like.

(1) MAKE HIM DEPENDENT ON YOU.

Take over a part of his busy life by doing it for him. This can be as simple as driving him around or cooking his meals or can involve more complexity like arranging his parties, sending out invitations (you can easily weed out unwanted competitors if you control the guest list) or helping to redecorate his summer house.

(2) SHOW HIM YOU ARE DEPENDENT ON HIM.

Ask his permission whenever you leave the house. Ask for his opinion on everything you do and wear. Show him he has your permission to be your boss.

(3) WRITE HIM LETTERS.

After he takes you on a weekend trip to Paris, write him long letters detailing the highlights of the trip. Write how much you enjoyed having tea at the Ritz and how good it felt to wake up next to him at the hotel. Tell him you are still sore from his fabulous lovemaking. And don't forget to remind him of all the things you did for him.

(4) PARROT BACK WHAT HE TELLS YOU.

Repeat his favorite phrases and aphorisms. Parroting his religious and political beliefs can be especially effective in making him think you are his soul mate. Use the exact language he uses in voicing these beliefs. The more narcissistic he is the more he will believe you are sincere.

(5) TAKE LOADS OF PICTURES.

Take pictures of him and send him the good ones with a flattering note about how "handsome" he looks, how his "charisma shines through" and how he truly "looks like a leader."

(6) COMPLIMENT HIM WHILE YOU LOOK AT HIM WITH EYES FILLED WITH ADMIRATION.

When he tells the same story for the 400th time, tell him how much you enjoy hearing it every time. Tell him he reminds you of his favorite person.

(7) DO WHAT HE WANTS–IMMEDIATELY.

When he asks you for something, get on it immediately. Don't ask him to do it and don't say, "I'll do it in a few minutes." Everything he asks you to do is an opportunity to please him.

(8) TELL HIM YOU WANT TO WRITE HIS BIOGRAPHY.

Show him how interested you are by making him tell you all about his life experiences and childhood growing up in New Jersey. Tape record him so "you can get a start on his biography" or just because you "want to have it to listen to." Tell him you want to write his biography so that others will be inspired by his achievements.

(9) ENCOURAGE HIM TO TELL YOU WHAT TO WEAR.

Ask him if he likes what you have on. Offer to change if he wants. Walk around barefoot or in sexy shoes and ask him if he likes your nail color. Sit on his lap and whisper how excited it makes you to be near him.

(10) SMILE AT HIM CONSTANTLY.

Remember–you love this job!

Advanced Bonding

Once you are in a serious relationship it's time for some advanced Gold Digging techniques. Here are some of the best.

Text Message him. Send him sweet and naughty messages all day long. Examples: "Sweetheart, I love you, sweetheart, I miss you, can't wait until you get home." Or tell him how much you have been doing for him or thinking about him while he is at work: "Honey, I took care of ordering the new couch–can't wait to sit on it with you. Call me about dinner. I made us a reservation at Le Cirque for Friday."

Plastic surgery. Get him to pay for it because it's for him. Have him choose and design your new breasts. They will be well worth the $4,000 each he will pay for them.

Financial arrangement. You must have a financial arrangement. Never spend your own money because it is always awkward to get reimbursed. Have him pay for everything. You never open your wallet. He should give you a credit card to charge whatever you need. Cabs take the petty cash. Better yet, make him get you an account at a car service.

Accept his cheating. Recognize that he is going to be occasionally unfaithful. If he is a player at heart he will love you if you tell him it's okay as long as he wears a condom, never tells you her last name and doesn't have any extended affairs.

Send him lists of things to do to make you happy. When you want him to buy something for you, send him a note with the URL and instructions on how to purchase it.

Block out his calendar far into the future. Plan things together for every single weekend all year around and don't forget holidays, birthdays and Valentine's Day. Throw in three one-week vacations every year. Plan these for him in detail so he has no free time except with you. When you et a good trip idea, don't wait. Tell him and then block out his calendar, all the travel agent and put the deposit down--on his credit card, ofcourse.

Act Engaged Even If You Aren't

Marriage must be assumed. Act committed. Act like a couple at all imes. Act engaged and he won't argue when the time comes. And start planning the wedding whether you are engaged or not. We know of one experienced Gold Digger who started wearing an engagement ring that her beau had not given her. Eventually he got used to the idea of being ngaged and now they are planning their wedding.

Have a back up plan. Don't put all your eggs in one basket. Keep a few other wealthy guys on the boil. Let them know gently that if your intended doesn't come through, you might give them a chance.

Take over every aspect of his life and make sure all his needs are taken care of. The housekeeper and secretary should report to you, not him. Make the grocery lists, pick out his ties, order his favorite wines for the house, pick all the restaurants for client dinners. Post your weekly schedule on the refrigerator for him and make sure his secretary has a copy. Organize his bills, answer his phone, open his mail and deal with his family. Put him on a diet and, if necessary, get him on antidepressants so he feels better around you. The only thing he should worry about is going to the office and making lots of money. For everything else, he should be completely dependent on you.

CHAPTER THIRTY-ONE

SEPARATING HIM FROM FRIENDS AND FAMILY

If you are unable to win over his friends or family, or if particular friend or family member is a sticking point, simpl sabotage his relationship with that person. Relationship sabotage can be delicate operation. To be successful, you will need to understand th basis for the relationship and what your guy and the other person each ge out of it.

Some relationships you just don't mess with. Sabotaging hi relationship with a spiteful child is suicide. Your man will almost alway care more about his children than you. The same is often, but not always true with parents. Parents and children are to be won over with attentio and generosity, not attacked.

The friends you want to get rid of are the womanizing colleg buddies, wing-men and colleagues at work, the ex-girlfriend who remain a confidante and occasion date, the hopeful girls he sees on the social se and any and all former and would be girlfriends. Other non-relatives who have slighted you are also appropriate targets.

Any social gaffe, selfish act, *faux pas* or insult uttered by the person you are trying to isolate should be remembered and used against him or her. Tell your target the story, always putting your enemy in the worst possible light. Imply that your enemy is just out for your man's money. Intimate that he or she doesn't care about your man at all. If your enemy is a woman, tell everyone that you suspect she has an eating disorder or an alcohol problem. Say that you heard she likes cocaine or crack. Say you overheard her purging in the ladies room. Tell your guy she dated his worst enemy.

Telling your guy that your female enemy is interested in him or that she is a nymphomaniac slut is dangerous. It could easily backfire by suddenly arousing his interest in sleeping with her. Make your rival seem creepy and neurotic instead.

CHAPTER THIRTY-TWO

HAVE HIS CHILDREN
(WHETHER HE LIKES IT OR NOT)

His Kids Are Your Key to Cash

The way to a man's wallet is through his children. Your Mr. Right might not care much about you. But he will care about the kids.

Once you have gotten pregnant, whether through marriage agreement, accident, trickery or out-right-fraud, you have finally got him by the balls.

Your child is your gold mine. No matter what the father does, you are likely going to get custody of the kids and he is going to have to pay you child support. Even if the judge hates you, even if you have been caught doing all kinds of horrible and embarrassing things, even if you don't get a penny of alimony or maintenance, you are going to get a generous amount for child support. This is true even if you have a tough pre-nuptial agreement.

Men may seem cold and uncaring. They may seem selfish or even evil. But they care about their kids.

For him, his children are him. Taking the kids is like taking him away from himself. He will howl in pain. That's why child custody battles are so fierce and vicious.

You are fighting for life and death here. His kids are his heirs. You can influence how his money gets spent through his children. The battle for the children can be the battle for the future of his property and estate. Never underestimate the value of having a child with your high net worth man. The child will keep you in his life for the rest of yours.

The quicker you get pregnant the better. Master the art of the inadvertent pregnancy.

Mastering the "Inadvertent" Pregnancy

Getting pregnant and having his child is the surest way possible to cement yourself like superglue to your guy of choice. The "inadvertent" pregnancy is a time-honored trick of high-end gold digging. Billionaire Steve Bing found this out the hard way when two very ambitious women (Lisa Bonder Kerkorian and Elizabeth Hurley) reportedly got pregnant from him in the space of a year, leaving him in a tangled mess of litigation.

Tell Him You're on the Pill

Claim you are taking birth control pills so he doesn't need to wear a condom. If he is smart enough not to trust you, leave your birth control pills lying around. Don't forget to take one out and flush it down the toilet every day. That way even if he checks he can see that you haven't forgotten to take your pill.

Punch Holes in All His Condoms

Rifle through his night table by the bed until you find his stash of condoms. Take a small sewing needle and prick several holes in each one. Then carefully replace them.

Steal His Sperm

Every time you have sex, you should view it as an opportunity to conceive his heir. If he doesn't believe you are on birth control and insists

on using a condom, wait until he is in the bathroom washing up after sex
Retrieve the condom from the garbage and hold it against your vagina
Then using your index finger press in on the tip of the condom and turn the
condom inside out while it is inside your vagina. Slosh it around until al
of the sperm has rubbed off inside of you. Remove the condom and rede
posit it in the trash. Then stand on your head for 10 minutes. With any
luck you have just created his sole heir.

Now then. Wasn't that easy?

Who says it's hard to get your hooks into a rich guy?

CHAPTER THIRTY-THREE

HOW TO BE A YOUNG WIDOW

Finding a wealthy man with one foot in the grave is the holy grail for the true Gold Digger. Men who are ill with cancer have many superior qualities. They are needy and vulnerable and often will not be able to perform basic tasks for themselves. And a man who is dying of prostate cancer (or almost anything else) will not be pressing you for sex. Move right in and take over his life. Help him with all his needs.

He is likely to think you are an angel sent to him by God as you run his errands, make all his arrangements and never overtly ask for anything in return. When he buys you presents, act overjoyed and tell him what a sweet, generous man he is. This will encourage him to give you more.

Spend lots of time alone with him. Read to him and massage him. Try to arrange a long trip with him. Take over his schedule and limit visits by close friends and family to the bare minimum.

"I'm afraid he really isn't up to seeing anyone today," should become your mantra.

Gradually you will break him down. Start telling him you want to be married to him so you can have the security to devote yourself 100% to his recovery.

Talk to his doctors and get the real story. Make sure you aren't dealing with a hypochondriac. Find out what is dangerous to him, things he should avoid and how long he can realistically go without medication.

Convince him to make a Living Will which states that no extraordinary medical procedures should be used to revive him in an emergency. Remind him to rethink the bequests in his Will. Make it clear how grateful you would be for anything he might do for you.

Be prepared for determined interference from friends and family. Strangely, the stronger and more powerful your sick mogul has been, the more vulnerable you are likely to find him when he is in ill health. This is because many truly successful men are highly narcissistic and really don't care about anyone but themselves. If you move in and devote yourself to such a man he will often throw his own children and lifelong friends aside and leave almost everything to you.

This was certainly the case with J.I., a Southern multi-millionaire, who married his wife's deathbed nurse two weeks after his wife died from Alzheimer's Disease. The nurse, an accomplished Gold Digger, who waited on J.I. hand and foot, not only married him but engineered a complete change in his Will, effectively disinheriting all of his children and grandchildren and leaving almost everything to herself. She accomplished this within a space of less than two years. And yes, J.I. actually told his children that the Gold Digging nurse was "an angel sent to him by God to care for him."

We love this stuff!

And don't forget to keep a potentially lethal bottle of sleeping pills (or, if you can get it, a nice supply of morphine) lying around in case hubby gets discouraged with his illness and wants to take his own life. Phenobarbital is a good choice. His swallowing 20 or 30 of those little pills should be enough to get you to the land of the free!

Key Documents

As a newlywed with a sick or aging husband, there are some very important documents you must keep track of or have in your possession. Your best bet is to keep them in your safety deposit box at the bank. In addition, make sure you have your safety deposit box key, marriage license, deeds to his houses, car documents, tax returns and receipts in a safe place. Check with his lawyers to ensure that every document is accounted for. And if you can't locate the title to one of the cars or the deed to one of the homes, begin the lengthy procedure of getting a duplicate while he's still alive.

A Copy of His Will. You must know where the original is kept. Obviously, you should lobby to become the prime beneficiary. Also try to convince him to appoint you as co-executor of the estate. This will give you some control over his assets almost immediately upon his death.

Living Will. This should provide that no extraordinary measures will be taken if he is near death. This will avoid the awkward situation of having hubby on a respirator in a coma for years while you are unable to inherit. Remember, you can't inherit his wealth until he is legally and irrevocably dead.

Health Care Proxy. This allows you to make all medical decisions on his behalf.

Social Security Card. You need the number for the death certificate and you can get widow's benefits if you don't remarry (although it probably won't be enough money to feed and groom your dog).

Bank Account Information. Move as much money as possible into accounts in your own name. Failing that, have the money in a joint account. While joint accounts are temporarily frozen upon death, they will go directly to you without passing through the estate.

Credit Cards and Account Numbers. You are not responsible for his credit card bills. Rack up as many charges as you can while he is still alive. It's the estate's problem, not yours.

Life Insurance Policies. You will want these in your possession. Life insurance is not part of the estate and goes directly to you if you are the beneficiary. That is, unless the police think you did him in.

Sperm Bank Documentation. If you haven't had children yet, don't despair. Daddy's death is no obstacle to having his children. Under New York law you can have his kids for up to three years after his death and the child will be an heir to the estate entitled to share in bequests. Check the law in your state. Get him to freeze his sperm as soon as he becomes severely ill and before the chemotherapy or radiation starts.

The Funeral. Last but not least, the estate pays for the funeral. Have a fabulous party to launch your social career as an independently wealthy woman. Invite 400 people for food, great wine, music and readings. Remember. He would have loved it!

CHAPTER THIRTY-FOUR

HIS CHILDREN AND PARENTS

His Children

The adult children of the High Net Worth Man are your natural enemies. You will be unlikely to find more feral and determined opponents.

His adult children will know or suspect exactly what you are up to. And they will know that they are the ones with the most to lose. From his adult children's perspective, just when it looked like the path to a clear inheritance from their mogul father was near, you stepped into the picture.

If you succeed in marrying him, the bulk or at least a large portion of his wealth (generally a minimum of one-third to one-half and even more if you convince him to employ certain estate planning techniques) will go to you. Your share will come directly out of the pockets of his adult children.

In addition, if you manage to have a child or two with their father, there will be even more mouths to feed at inheritance time. His children know you want to have children if you can, if only to secure your continued involvement and financial commitment in case their father divorces you.

These circumstances will make his adult children a determined enemy. Do not trust his children. They will be lobbying strongly against your marriage behind your back. Any mistakes you make can and will be used against you.

Any social *faux pas*, poor choice of words or wardrobe, indication of negative feelings toward their father or them or their friends and relatives will be immediately reported to your mogul as definitive proof of your bad character and evil intentions.

Kill Them with Kindness; Smother Them with Warmth

An outright battle with his children will generally be a losing proposition. Your only good course of action is likely to be to try to win them over. Charm them, involve them in your activities, buy them presents, convey to them how much you love their father and them. And don't give them anything negative they can report to your target.

Make the children understand that you understand their position. Take no overt steps against them now. After you are married there will be plenty of time to get his Will changed in your favor.

In spite of all this, his children may remain implacable foes. But if you play it correctly they will be without ammunition against you.

Small Children

Small children can generally be won over with attention, kindness and presents. Don't interfere with your divorced man's time with his small children. You will make both father and children into enemies if you do. Take the kids to the park or the zoo. Take them to the toy store. Buy them a bunny rabbit. If you are attentive and involved you will win them over. And your mogul will take notice.

His Parents

Parents are tricky. As long as they don't control the purse strings you can breathe easy. It is not likely that they will be in a position to block your path. But don't take any chances. If possible, you want them affirmatively on your side.

Parents generally want two things: maximum continued involvement with their successful son and grandchildren. They may also want some money, but generally not in quantities that will affect its availability to you.

Inherited Wealth

One Sotheby's real estate broker told us that she doesn't date men with inherited wealth. As she said of one unemployed scion of a wealthy New York family, "Jack was very fortunate that his father was born before he was." Men who inherit their money are often lacking in drive and direction. "They're wimps," said our lovely broker. "They may be good at golf or tennis but they aren't sexy. Power is what turns me on. And that is what you get with a man who has made it on his own."

While this girl's approach is not for everybody, it is important to keep in mind that many men with so called inherited wealth, haven't inherited it yet. Someone else may still control the purse strings. And men with inherited wealth often feel insecure about their abilities since they usually didn't do anything to deserve their inheritance.

Inherited wealth is a different market because you may have many more family constituencies to please (including "Purse String Parents" described below), than you would with a self-made mogul. However, many socially adept women thrive amidst inherited wealth.

And sometimes inherited wealth can lead to certain eccentricities, like riding around your property on a tank, something John DuPont IV was particularly fond of doing before he was taken away by the nice men in the white suits.

Inherited money. It's your move.

Purse String Parents

Parents who control the purse strings present an entirely different set of problems. In fact, you will have to carefully consider whether you even want to go there.

Purse String Parents may feel they have the right to choose their son's mate. And since they control the cash flow, effectively they do. Purse String Parents usually have kept control of the purse strings either because they are very controlling parents or because their son is completely irresponsible with money. Or it may have been done precisely to prevent him from marrying a gold digger.

The first step in dealing with Purse String Parents is to find out the actual situation.

How much of an income is your target getting?

Can it be cut off at any time or is there an irrevocable trust?

Is there a specific time at which he will come into his money or is that in the discretion of his parents or someone else?

Then ask yourself, can you live with the risks built into his inheritance structure?

In many cases, the answer will be No and you will have to cut your losses and move on.

Keep in mind that this situation is made even more difficult by the fact that Purse String Parents are generally highly focused on preventing their son from marrying a gold digger. They will be cold and dispassionate in working to get you out of their son's life if they suspect you might be one.

Winning Over the Parents

Whatever kind of parents he has, there are some well established techniques for winning them over.

Pay attention to them. Make sure they come for the holidays. Go with him when he visits them. Arrange to do things with his mother. Be helpful around the house when you visit them. Tell them how wonderful their son is and what wonderful parents they must be to have produced such a terrific son. Buy them presents on their birthdays and on Mother's and Father's Day. Send them notes so they feel involved in your relationship with their son. Take his parents out to dinner at least every 4-6 months. If you are lucky they will insist on paying the bill.

If he has no children, tell his parents that you look forward to having kids and to their involvement in raising them. Tell them how important your grandparents were to you and that you want the same thing for your children.

If he has children already, show his parents how good you are with them and how much of an asset you can be.

All of these efforts help disarm a potential natural enemy. If you do well, you may even be able to use his parents as allies in winning over his adult children.

Negativism is a No-No

Be positive when you talk about his parents with him. Being on the wrong side of family quarrels creates the potential for disaster. Don't be negative about his parents to him and don't ever be negative about him to his parents or children.

In family matters, as in other things, negativity is a big, big no-no.

CHAPTER THIRTY-FIVE

THE GOLD DIGGERS HALL OF FAME:
10 GIRLS WHO MADE IT TO THE TOP

The Deathbed Nurse

The lovely D. nursed the husband's dying wife for several years. The wife had Alzheimer's Disease. She had been married to a Mississippi businessman for more than 50 years. D. worked as a live-in nurse for the wife. Within two weeks of the wife's death, she married the husband with whom she had secretly been carrying on an affair for many months. D. did whatever the husband told her to do, wore what he told her to wear and walked the way he told her to walk. She repeatedly told him he was "a genius." The husband told everyone how D. was "sent by God to give joy to his life."

D. soon began working on disinheriting the husband's three children so that everything would go to her when her husband died. Her husband recently obliged by passing away at the age of 87. The husband's three children were so intimidated by their narcissistic patriarch that they didn't dare confront him about D. D. succeeded in getting what she wanted by giving her husband everything he wanted. Now she owns everything he owned.

The Guru

N. has somewhat mysterious origins but claims to be "from France." She is stunningly beautiful, highly intelligent, direct, with the calmness, charm and feeling of wholeness of a guru. She has tremendous personal power. She is not a classic Gold Digger. But still in her late 30s, she is younger than her two stepdaughters and more than 40 years younger than her wealthy husband. Her husband was previously married to an Eastern European princess. One of "his" daughters looks nothing like him and has been rumored to be the product of a well documented affair between the princess and President John F. Kennedy. The other daughter was a successful television star who was married to Hollywood's most notorious aging producer for two weeks. N. is a magnificent woman. She could capture any man's heart but is such a superior being that it is difficult for any woman to learn lessons from her. N. is a woman who landed a wealthy guy because she deserved him. She adds as much value to her husband's life as he does to hers.

Paula Fortunato

Forty-year-old schoolteacher Paula Fortunato married 79-year-old Sumner Redstone in April 2003 after meeting him on a blind date in New York City. Redstone is Chairman and CEO and largest shareholder of the parent company of Viacom which owns Paramount Pictures, CBS, MTV and Simon & Schuster among many other holdings. Several years previously the notorious Robert Evans had invited several women to his home in Los Angeles to meet Redstone. Redstone made a beeline for then top movie acquisition executive Anne Templeton. Says Templeton, who now owns a yoga studio in Hobe Sound, "There were some B movie actresses and the usual bimbos hanging around Evans and I had headed straight to the corner and sat down trying to hide," says Templeton. "He came right to me and we had a great conversation but I snuck out at the first opportunity. Redstone is badly scarred [from burns he received while hanging from a ledge outside a burning building in Boston many years ago] and I just couldn't see myself marrying a half burned man." The fortunate Ms. Fortunato is likely to end up with a fortune worth billions when that lucky burn victim passes on to that great movie in the sky. As for Ms. Templeton, she is now dating a retired multi-millionaire from Jupiter Island. So in this story everybody lived happily ever after.

Dr. Laurie Perlman

Forty-nine-year-old Laurie Perlman has proved that you can still pick up a guy with a few bucks after 45. She landed former AOL Time Warner CEO Gerald Levin notwithstanding Levin's 32 year marriage to Barbara Levin. Perlman, who is a clinical psychologist, reeled in Levin in early 2003 after meeting him through her efforts to create a network of holistic mental health institutions. Levin, who had had a mentally retarded sister who died when he was six-years-old, fell for Perlman and sealed their engagement in early 2003 with an emerald and diamond engagement ring. Unfortunately for her, by this time, because of the collapse of AOL-Time Warner's stock, his net worth had reportedly declined below $10 million.

Patricia Ward Kelly

Patricia Ward married Hollywood dance and film legend Gene Kelly when he was 77 and she was 36. Patricia took over his schedule and used her authority to cut-off his family and friends. Using two strokes as a pretext, Patricia systematically eliminated Kelly's support system, eliminating his secretary of 50 years and firing his business manager, lawyer and doctor. Friends' calls were not returned and Patricia even banned Kelly's children from staying at his house during the funeral. She had Kelly's body cremated before even informing his children of their father's death. Of course, she also managed to get the Will changed and ended up inheriting virtually all of his money with Kelly's children getting almost nothing.

Shoshanna Lonstein

The big bosomed fashion designer landed Joshua Gruss heir of the mega-wealthy Martin Gruss fortune in May 2003. Foiled by fellow hall of fame gold digger Jessica Sklar in landing her previous boyfriend, Jerry Seinfeld, this gold digging prodigy has now married into even greater wealth than Seinfield could muster. Knowing Shoshanna, we feel she has what it takes to navigate the perils of inherited wealth with her young scion. And she got a husband who is only two years older than she. At 27, Shoshanna already shows the maturity and poise to make our Hall of Fame. Great gold digging Shoshanna!

Heather Mills

Who says you can't gold dig on one leg? Handicapped Heather Mills is an inspiration to all ambitious women. This formerly homeless, hop-along Cassidy of English Gold Digging started out dating a rich Lebanese businessman while she was still married to former husband Alfie Karmal. Notwithstanding losing her left leg in a 1993 collision with a police motorcycle, she leveraged herself into marriage with ex-Beatle Paul McCartney. The sappy crooner still swears by his one-legged spouse in spite of numerous press reports of her power gold digging exploits. Heather, who boasts one of the only open-toed leg prostheses in England, is our own Hall of Fame Gold Digging Special Olympics champion. We wish her well.

Elesbeth Gillet – Cutthroat Gold Digging

Elesbeth Ingalls Gillet makes our Hall of Fame with an over-the-top brassiness that would make our other honorees blush with shame. Mrs. Gillet, who resides at the former Gillet family Palm Beach estate, Pelican Hall, is the widow of F. Warrington Gillet, Jr. of the Gillette razor Gillets. Her late husband, or "Big Warry" as he was known to his widow, died under mysterious circumstances at Pelican Hall in May 2002. Family members are still trying to get the body exhumed. Needless to say, "Big Warry" left everything to Eles who was less than generous with the rest of the family. How ungenerous? Well they got nothing. *Bupkus*. Not even "Big Warry's" son, "Little Warry". Asked to comment on the dispute with the family, Mrs. Gillet told *The New York Observer's* George Gurley that "There's nothing to work out. I'm happy to talk to him, ["Little Warry" who was completely disinherited by Big Warry's will] but the will was written as it was, and that's it. I'm not going to break the will myself, especially because everything was left to me!" Of her stepson, she told Gurley, "I gave him 10 or 12 suits. There was more to come but not now. I had a ring I was going to give him that belonged to his father. But to heck with it. I had it cut down, and it fits my little pinky finger now."

Some might think Mrs. Gillet a tad selfish. But if a woman doesn't take care of herself, who will?

Great gold digging Eles!

Julia Fletcher Koch and Lisa Kittredge – The Miracle of Prostate Cancer

Our last two hall-of-famers benefited greatly from weakness induced by the miracle of prostate cancer.

Julia Fletcher had campaigned unsuccessfully for Texas oil billionaire David Koch for several years while she struggled to pay the rent on her one bedroom apartment in Manhattan. Julia finally got her man after he was diagnosed with prostate cancer and is now an important society hostess.

Lisa Kittredge landed smelly candle mogul Michael Kittredge, founder of The Yankee Candle Company, the old fashioned way–by working as his assistant. While helping out her man at work, Lisa also found time for extracurricular activities with the captain of Kittredge's magnificent 200 foot superyacht, the Paraffin. Kittredge, like Koch, finally threw in the towel and married the lucky Lisa after she nursed him through his bout with prostate cancer.

What is it about the miracle of prostate cancer that puts men in marriage mode? That's easy. Since the treatment for the disease almost always involves long periods of impotence, men lose the ability to carry on shagging loads of attractive women. They start thinking about other things that rarely enter the minds of healthy men–like their future, and who is going to take care of them when they are sick and can't get it up anymore. These thoughts usually have a salutary effect on a man's relationship with his girlfriend. This goes to prove one of our most useful Gold Digger adages–"His weaknesses are your opportunities."

So send your intended off for a complete physical check-up. And make sure they include a test for prostate cancer. Even if your man is healthy, try getting your doctor to tell him he isn't.

You will be amazed at the results!

Honorable mention to Patricia Duff for dumping Mike Medavoy and marrying and divorcing Ron Perelman. Patricia is now dating Arthur Altschul.

Way to go Patricia!

On the "his weaknesses are your opportunities" front, our final honoree–let's call her M.R.–must remain nameless.

M.R. pulled off a major coup when she married D.S., a mentally retarded centi-millionaire in the Hamptons. While playing with LEGO blocks may not be your idea of an ideal afternoon with your husband, we are pretty sure that M.R. is laughing all the way to the cash machine.

PART FIVE

High Net Worth Dating Pitfalls

CHAPTER THIRTY-SIX

WHAT YOU'RE UP AGAINST

" Any man who wants to get married is too dumb to live with," says one particularly insightful Gold Digger.

Getting married is almost never in a wealthy man's interest. You will have your work cut out for you, when you try to wrangle that engagement ring out of him. Landing a high net worth husband isn't easy. It's hard work that requires dedication, persistence and careful planning. In the early stages, a wrong move, unplanned temper tantrum or embarrassing remark in front of his friends can disturb the rhythm of your relationship to the point where he loses interest. Once lost, interest is rarely regained.

You may have made a great impression on the first date. You may have had four great dates in a row. Don't get lightheaded. You are still a long way from an engagement ring.

Sally, an uptown socialite, kept running into the same handsome bachelor at event after event. He would always come over to say hello. Each time he introduced himself and asked her name and they would have a great conversation. The trouble was that he obviously had no idea that he had met her before. He even took Sally's number twice but never called. She was crushed. The guy liked her every time he saw her but could not remember who she was for more than a few hours.

Herein lies an important secret of dating very wealthy or attractive men. They meet lots of women. So many in fact that keeping track of all the names and phone numbers can become a logistical nightmare.

One downtown high net worth bachelor named Andrew told us, "I've got drawers filled with scraps of papers with phone numbers on them. I have legal pads stacked on my dresser with hundreds of names and numbers. My cell phone has long ago been filled up. I have no idea who 99% of these women are."

Men who are active on the social circuit can meet three or four eligible beauties every night. They come home with stacks of business cards and pieces of paper.

"When I clean out my wallet, briefcase and pockets at the end of the week and find 10 phone numbers, I already will have forgotten who half the women are when I go to put their numbers into my computer or phone book," says Andrew.

While Andrew is a particularly handsome and charming bachelor, the problems he faces are experienced by many wealthy men. When they are deciding whom to date they have to look through lists of women whose names may mean nothing to them.

They are not going to ask you out unless they somehow remember who you are.

Many women sit at home steaming because a guy who took their number at a party didn't call. No need to get angry. In some cases he will have lost your phone number or doesn't know which phone number is yours. If you like him and have his business card but he hasn't called you, send him an e-mail reminding him who you are. Other times it will take a second or third encounter before he calls. And if he doesn't call you, he doesn't exist.

Here are some other tricks for getting him to remember you. When you meet a high net worth man it is useful to have some piece of information that you are going to get for him or that he is going to get for you that will force the two of you into communication again in the near future regardless of whether he calls to ask you out.

Start Off Doing Him a Favor

Perhaps you or he has an apartment or job tip for one another. Maybe he has a friend who wants to meet one of your girlfriends. Maybe you know a social event, charitable cause, wonderful restaurant in Provence or Tuscany or a great place to stay in St. Barths. Try to think of something while you are talking to him that will require you to speak with him again. Offering to be helpful about something he is interested in, like finding a house in Palm Beach for the winter, going to a party or being hooked up with a business or social connection is often the best approach. Go out of your way to do him a favor and he will remember you.

Arrange a Chance Encounter

When you meet a guy you like he will generally give you his business card. Quickly scan the address and ask him where he likes to have lunch in that neighborhood during the week. This may give rise to a lunch invitation. If it doesn't, you now know where he likes to have his midday meal.

Allow a decent interval to pass (at least a week) and arrange a lunch date with a friend at one of his favorite restaurants. Since men are creatures of habit, if you do this a few times, you will eventually run into him.

If you find out where he likes to go on weekends you can do the same thing in the country. Maybe he is divorced and likes to take his little boy to the Candy Kitchen in Bridgehampton for breakfast on Saturdays. If you are in The Hamptons anyway, there is no harm in driving by the Candy Kitchen and stopping in to see if your target is there on your way to exercise class.

Arranging a chance encounter is another weapon in your arsenal that you can use to get in touch with your target without having to call him. Such encounters often lead to the next date and beyond. It isn't stalking, it's just common sense.

If He Doesn't Call, He Doesn't Exist

If a tree falls in the forest and no one hears it, does it make a sound? This question has vexed sophomoric minds for generations.

We don't know the answer either. But we do know that if a man does not call you, he does not exist.

Don't waste time worrying about non-existent guys who don't call you. They don't matter. Get out there and find guys who will call you.

It is pointless to wait by the phone for a call. You can worry about your guy when he calls you. Until then you have plenty of work to do creating interest in other High Net Worth guys who will call you. This is the proactive solution to guys who don't call.

Let them figure out how to emerge from limbo. Let them figure out how to get back into the game. It's not your problem. You only consider suitors who call you.

When your girlfriend asks you, "Has Fred called you lately?"

There is only one answer.

"Who's Fred?"

CHAPTER THIRTY-SEVEN

HIGH NET WORTH DATING PITFALLS

As with every important goal worth achieving, the path to landing a high net worth husband is a minefield of obstacles. That's why you need this handy guide to work your way past the pitfalls that await every ambitious woman.

Toxic Bachelors and Husbands

One of the most dangerous environmental hazards you will face on your quest for a life of easy luxury is the toxic bachelor. These party animals date half a dozen women at the same time and may go through a hundred or more women in a year's time.

Why do they behave in this boorish and disloyal fashion? That's easy. Because they can.

These guys thrive because the number of lovely young women on the high net worth dating circuit greatly outnumbers the wealthy available men. Some of these guys have been around for decades. And they know what to say to cover their tracks.

Many of them will walk in talking about marriage and children, their houses in Palm Beach and Southampton, how they are thinking of buying a plane and how much they like to stay home with their girlfriend. They appear rich and well connected. They are charming. You will see them at every important party.

And they are liars.

These guys know just what to say to win our hearts. They are pros. They have been doing it for years. The only problem is that most of what they tell us is not true.

Your task is to identify the toxic bachelors on the scene and avoid them like the plague.

The best way to avoid TBs is to ask around. Do your background checks. Talk to the old-time gold diggers ("OTGDs") who are in their late 30s (or wish they were) who are still working the scene. OTGDs are priceless sources. They can probably get you the skinny on almost any of these guys. Don't believe what your date is telling you until you have checked it with another source.

The benefit circuit attracts toxic men because that's one of the principal places they find girls. TBs look at every young girl who comes to a party as fresh meat. TBs are at every party. They love parties. If you see a guy at too many parties, check him out carefully. Most likely he is a TB. Talk to as many people as you can at the parties. You never know where it might lead. By asking any OTGD these questions, you can make a master list of TBs to avoid as well as learning other important business targeting information, like which high net worth individuals have recently split with their girlfriends, separated from their wives and whose marriage looks like it may end up on the rocks.

The High Net Worth Sex Addict

High net worth men who date too much can become sex addicts. This is more common than you would think. It sometimes occurs in men who are addicted to other things like alcohol or cocaine. One well-known rock star who must remain anonymous (let's call him B.J.) suffers from this disease.

Driving around one night in his limo, B.J. spotted a tall, thin blonde walking under an umbrella in the rain. He stopped and offered her a ride. "When she got in I could see she had teeth like a horse," said a girlfriend who was present. "I'll buy her new teeth," was B.J.'s response. This girl, who was Russian, spoke little English and never revealed her last name. She would only meet B.J. on the street. He never found out anything about her, yet he was madly in love with her and bought her loads of jewelry.

"Spoil us and we become monsters," said another thirty-something gold digger. "The more things he bought me the more I had to have. The jewelry became like an addiction."

But with most sex addicts you won't have this problem. The high net worth sex addict just wants to sleep with you and move on to the next girl. He does not want to buy you jewelry. He will get tired of you immediately after he has sex with you. He may even try to get you to leave right after sex in order to avoid having to spend the entire night with you. Sex addicts will even go to group therapy sessions to pick up girls. Sex addicts are not going to marry you, and if they do they are going to cheat on you relentlessly.

Some high net worth men become sex addicts because sex with multiple partners is so easily available to them. Rock stars, film stars and very good looking multi-millionaires are particularly prone to this affliction. The last thing on these players' minds is marrying you.

Avoid these hyperactive sex machines. Stick with your plain, old, short, fat, boring, balding billionaire and you can't go wrong. Go after a young Charlie Sheen type and you will get what you deserve. You will get fucked.

Overexposure

Overexposure comes from too much time on the benefit circuit. Your best chances of landing a rich man are when you are still fresh in your first two years on the scene.

After a couple of years or even sooner if you go to too many similar events, you will become overexposed. Overexposed gold diggers can be the subject of contempt from high net worth males. Look around at the big parties. You will see a consistent sprinkling of women in their mid to late 30s and early 40s. They rarely have the same date more than two or three events in a row. They may once have been very beautiful. But they have already dated most of the players on the circuit. They are no longer highly prized dating material. As their dating careers spiral downward, they tend to go for more and more plastic surgery. Gradually they become unrecognizable. Still youthful seeming, but everyone who counts knows the truth. Word about them quickly spreads among high net worth males.

Soon the OTGDs won't be able to find dates at all.

So strike while you are still thin and wrinkle free. Strike while your skin still has that glowing elasticity of youth. Strike now or risk living in purgatory as an OTGD.

Get What You Can While You Can

"Sweetie, you've got to snap them up as soon as they get divorced," Candace Bushnell urged her friend, writer Kate Bohner. Candace had wanted Kate to go after AOL honcho Bob Pittman who had just divorced Sandy Pittman. Kate had been seated next to him at a dinner party and the two had had great conversation. Candace thought Kate should move immediately. Her position was that you can't let the ball bounce too many times on the rebound. "Sweetie, guys like that get snapped up right away. Go for it." Of course she was right. Pittman was grabbed up almost immediately by Veronica Choa.

Make What You Want Known

Being shy won't get you there. Believe us when we tell you that Sally Quinn isn't married to *Washington Post* publisher Ben Bradlee because she is shy. This brassy and ostentatious lady made her play for Bradlee by tendering her resignation to him. She marched into his office and announced that she was resigning because "I'm head over heels in love with you and I just can't work here anymore." Bradlee easily convinced the super ambitious Quinn to stay. They have now been married for almost 20 years. A family source indicates that Quinn is as tough as ever and has been on a non-stop campaign since the wedding to separate Bradlee from his children by a previous marriage. More power to her!

What If You Get Dumped?

Most women don't understand that when a high net worth man dumps you, it is rarely personal. He has usually found someone who amuses him more. When the press stories hit that Kate Bohner's husband, writer Michael Lewis, author of *Liar's Poker,* had been having an affair with Tabitha Soren, Candace Bushnell's reaction was classic.

"Sweetie, at least you married someone famous. Nobody can take that away from you."

When the deluge of publicity about her husband's affair hit, Candace's response was "Sweetie, you played it great. You're a scorned woman. It makes him look bad."

"This is my life you are talking about Candace–not a press story," said Kate. But Candace didn't see the difference. And from her perspective she was right. Kate's marriage was over. But the good news was that she had come out well in the press.

CHAPTER THIRTY-EIGHT

THE 10 BIGGEST MISTAKES
YOU CAN MAKE

The conquest of the high net worth male is an elaborate chess game filled with many possibilities for error along the way. It is remarkable how many intelligent glamorous women can be blinded by their own ambition and end up being cast aside because they overlooked a few easy to remember rules.

THE 10 BIGGEST MISTAKES

(1) Don't fight with his family.

He has known his family longer than he has known you. No matter what his relationship with his parents, siblings, ex-wives and adult children, there is no upside for you to antagonize them. Without some in depth study, you are unlikely to figure out all the dynamics of his family relationships until after you are married. Before you are married you can't afford to make enemies of his family members.

(2) Don't yell at him, especially in public.

Men do not like to be shamed. If you humiliate him publicly in restaurants or in front of friends or family, you will not be in the running for long.

(3) Don't keep him waiting too long.

One of the biggest complaints men have about women is that they take too long to leave the house. His waiting for you is not proof of his love for you, but it will be proportional to his annoyance at you. He will be very grateful if you are on time and show consideration for his extremely busy schedule. Don't lord it over him by being constantly late.

(4) Don't be annoying.

Numerous phone calls at work can be extremely annoying. Your guy is at work to make money for you. Don't get in his way by calling to discuss trivial matters or demand affection and attention. He is not in the office to wile away his day gabbing with you. Remember he is a boyfriend, not a girlfriend. Every communication with him should have a purpose. When you have accomplished it get off the phone.

(5) Don't lay out cash for your own expenses and then ask to be reimbursed.

Have him give you a credit card, but don't ask him for cash. Asking for cash will make him suspicious of your motives. Manipulate him to allow you to charge your expenses on his credit card. A woman who is whining for cash is far from an attractive sight. Many high net worth men are surprisingly stingy. If you press them for cash, you are pressing their buttons in a way that will not have long-term benefits for you.

(6) Don't let him into your apartment.

If you are living in a studio apartment, dorm room, single occupancy hotel or anywhere else that screams "modest means" keep your boyfriend away from your apartment. The shock of seeing how you live puts far too much focus on the difference between your economic status and his. It cannot help but make him suspicious. Meet him at the restaurant or meet him at his place. But keep him away from your fold out couch and near empty refrigerator.

(7) Don't tell him about the details of your diet or beauty regimen.

Your mogul wants a beautiful woman. He does not care how you get that way or how much better you look now than before. Don't tell him how much weight you have lost. He will simply assume that you will eventually put all those pounds back on. Don't tell him about your pedicure and manicure or how much your wax job hurt. He does not care. He just wants you to look good. He does not want to know the details. And don't talk about your period unless you have to. It's not his problem.

(8) Don't go psycho.

Many women self-destruct by letting their frustrations explode in anger at their boyfriend. Just because you've been dating for nine months and he hasn't given you an engagement ring is no reason to wake him up in the morning by throwing ashtrays at his head. Needless to say, do not stalk him or boil his pet rabbit, cat or dog in a pot on the stove. Keep your emotions in check. Letting yourself boil over can be fatal to your relationship building efforts.

(9) Do not be totally enamored of him.

You are going to be with this guy for a long time. You had better start liking him. If you are not in love, pretend to be. And do not criticize him or tell him he is wrong. He will not want to hear that under any circumstances. Boyfriends are repelled when you criticize them. Don't be negative about him or anything else. Tell him he is the king of your world. Nothing will build trust better than if you are continually positive in what you say about your feelings for him. Don't criticize him behind his back to your girlfriends. They are more likely to use your indiscretions against you than they are to sympathize with your plight.

(10) Beware of the First Wives Club.

As a young glamour girl, to his friends' wives, you are the enemy. You represent everything they fear most. You are a symbol of what could happen to them. When a man dumps his wife for a younger woman, the new woman should not expect to be welcomed with open arms by his friends' and colleagues' wives. They will be terrified that their husbands will follow your guy's example and dump them too. To preserve their own position they will have to bad mouth you to their husbands. Don't take it personally. These women are fighting for their lives. They see you as their own replacement. And they won't want you near their husbands under any circumstances.

Don't Bring Your Problems Home from Work

If, notwithstanding our advice, you have kept your high pressure day job, do not burden your man with your problems at work. Your problems are not his problems. He has plenty of problems of his own. He won't want to hear about yours. While there is no harm in asking for advice on a specific problem, generalized complaints about your job will make him feel irritable and hopeless about you. In general men would prefer to think that you can solve your own problems, whether or not this is the truth.

CHAPTER THIRTY-NINE

ALL THAT GLITTERS IS NOT CASH

Avoiding the Impoverished Socialite

Among the many land mines you will have to avoid on the path to wealth and happiness, is a breed of useless bachelors who don't have the goods but may appear to.

Do your research before getting involved with a new bachelor. Just because he looks good, dresses well, works on Wall Street and you met him at Tara Rockefeller's cocktail party does not mean he meets the Minimum Net Wealth Standard. Like the toxic bachelors, married men cheating on their wives, drug dealers, serial killers and organized crime members on the dating circuit, these guys may look like the real thing but they are not.

Don't Date Men Who Live Below the "Poverty Line"

They may once have had some money and lost it in a business reversal or expensive divorce. They may have been fired from a lucrative investment banking position. Or they may have wealthy parents who won't allow them a penny of their own money. Often they are from the poor branch of a wealthy family or else are struggling professionals trying to get by on $300,000 to $500,000 a year in a finance job. In any event, they live below the $500,000 per year "poverty line." Not nearly enough to support the kind of lifestyle you would like to become accustomed to. They may have enough money to squire you around town and take you out to an occasional upscale restaurant meal. But they don't have the cash to buy you the essential jewelry, clothes, vacations and houses you need.

These guys can be useful as Walkers and as social connections to introduce you to other people, but they are not appropriate people for you to date. If you suspect that a man who interests you may be an impoverished socialite, find out through your girl network where he lives. Talk to someone who has been to his apartment. Ask them what it is like. Does he own or rent? Sometimes you can get clues from the guy himself. Does he own a summer house? What kind of car does he keep in the city? With careful research and analysis you can easily avoid most impoverished bachelors.

One attractive and high profile real estate broker we know (let's call her "P") was seated next to a very charming and sexy European named Eric at a dinner party in Southampton. By the time the dinner plates had been removed he had worked her into a tizzy. He whispered into her ear as they were waiting for dessert, "Go take off your panties in the ladies room."

Nearly mad with desire, P rushed to the ladies room to do as she was told. Breathless, she ran into the hostess on the way back. P could not contain herself. "Do you know Eric? He's so handsome."

The hostess smiled. "P, I doubt you want to go there. Eric hasn't got a pot to pee in."

P stopped in her tracks. "Really?" She paused. "How bad is it?"

"Studio apartment near Columbia University."

"Oh dear," muttered P as she scurried back to the bathroom to replace her panties.

P was last seen leaving the party mumbling "studio apartment" in horror under her breath.

Be High Net Worthy

You are a skinny, scrumptious, sexy woman. If you rigorously follow the tips in this book and our recommended exercise program, high net worth boyfriends will be salivating over you. You will be eye candy they want to keep.

You are not doing this for free. Your dates must be made to understand that you are a girl in demand. If he doesn't come through with gifts of jewelry, cars, vacations in Aspen, Palm Beach, St. Barths and St. Tropez, punish him.

Your absence should be sufficient to generate a lucrative flurry of attention. Don't return his calls for a week. When he is calling you in a frenzy tell him to take you shopping.

If he says no, dump him. You cannot afford stingy suitors.

CHAPTER FORTY

WATCH OUT FOR THE CHARMERS

You've met a tall, handsome, athletic looking investment banker in his early 40s. Divorced with no children, he has just told you about his houses in Palm Beach and Southampton and invited you for dinner next week at The Four Seasons restaurant. You have given him your home phone number. You begin to imagine yourself in the South of France getting married at the Hotel du Cap in a Vera Wang wedding dress.

Then the reports start trickling in. Your friend Sabrina dated him but won't talk. The background check comes back with the word WOMANIZER! in block capital letters.

Yet at dinner you forget all that. He is so charming, so well-dressed and well-mannered, so solicitous of your every need. He remembers what you like to eat and orders it for you. He smiles and takes your hand across the table. You are leaning across the table already looking forward to the first kiss.

Put on the brakes. You are not the first woman he has made to feel that way. You might not even be the five hundredth. You are at risk of being another of his three week wonders.

Don't fall into his arms. Don't show him he is pushing on an open door. Be engaged and amusing but don't let him go too far with the good night kiss. Show him you are different than the others and he'll have to work hard to get you.

In the meantime you are gathering information. Use the dinner conversation to find out who his friends are (get their full names), where he goes on vacation and when, where he works, and the names of any important colleagues. Find out if he has any club memberships. You will then need to follow up each of these clues with more legwork to properly asses his value to you and your future.

Ask to go out with him together with his guy friends. Get to know the girls who are dating those friends. They can give you the real story. Find an excuse to call him on his cell phone at night and ask him where he is. Leave a sexy message on his home phone number in the evening. Mail panties anonymously to his apartment.

All the while you are learning whether he has ever been in a serious relationship. Is he a sex addict or alcoholic? How is he really doing at work? Is he dating anyone else? If so, how many other girls are there on his rotation?

Within a few weeks you should have a complete file on your target.

CHAPTER FORTY-ONE

BEWARE THE STINGY SWELL

"All the guys I date are high net worth," said one prominent New York magazine editor. "The problem is they spend so much time worrying about whether I'm after their money that they end up being stingy just to test me."

"One Christmas I spent a fortune on some beautiful cufflinks for David and he bought me a cheap silver bracelet from Tiffany's. I broke up with him soon after, but I couldn't stand looking at that bracelet. So I took it back and upgraded it for something I had always wanted."

The cheap multi-millionaire is the scourge of the high net worth dating circuit. Amanda Ross, daughter of billionaire Wilbur Ross, has a story of one such guy. "My friend Chris who has millions wanted me to take him to the mechanic in Southampton where I have my car repaired because it's difficult to get an appointment unless they know you. I said I would drive over with him in the morning. Chris said, 'Great but you have to drive me back in the afternoon to pick up the car.' I said, I had plans.

Chris said, 'In that case you have to pay for my taxi'. He argued with me until I gave him $20."

The stingy man is acting out of anxiety about money. Stingy men usually have difficulty loving or bonding with others. Stingy men usually do not make good husbands. If you don't mind a stingy husband, marry someone who is already poor not someone who is afraid of being poor.

Of course stingy men can be broken. They usually have a weakness that they are dying for you to exploit. If you can get a stingy man to open his heart, you may find that he is stingy with everyone but you.

The stingy man is typically narcissistic and fear ridden. Use the bonding techniques described in Chapter 30 to break down his resistance If that doesn't work, dump him.

CHAPTER FORTY-TWO

YOUR GIRLFRIENDS ARE THE ENEMY

Your Girlfriends Are Not Your Friends

Every successful gold digger girl knows that her girlfriends are out for themselves. Don't leave your girlfriends alone with your potential fiancés. You may run into them at the gym one day sporting a big rock from the guy you wanted.

Girlfriends are good for discussing fashion tips, social events, gossip, sample sales and your boyfriend's weird behavior. They are not good for introducing to your boyfriend. If you are forced to take your man to dinner with your girlfriends make sure they also bring dates. If one of them flirts with your Mr. Right, put your foot down hard on her toes. Don't give your guy an opening either. After the dinner go through his wallet checking for your girlfriends' business cards. Remove and destroy any you find.

Give Him One Before He Leaves the House

One excellent pre-dinner precaution when you know that you are going to a social function where there will be female competition is to give your guy a blow job before he leaves the house. This simple procedure can keep his mind off other women for periods of up to 90 minutes and should also be incorporated into your preparations whenever you go out without him or whenever he goes out without you.

There is nothing like self-preservation for your pre-dinner appetizer.

Sharpen Your Knives – Watch for Backstabbing Opportunities

Never trust your girlfriends, but watch for weaknesses in their relationships. One girl's break up can be another girl's dream-come-true. Get your girlfriends to confide in you. Make them tell you all the problems they are having with their boyfriends. Getting your girlfriends to pour their heart out is easy. All you have to do is stand next to them.

If she is dating someone you are interested in, have a drink with her or call her on the phone. Everything normally spews out like an undigested meal within 30 minutes. This information download should give you all the relevant data you need to eventually steal her high net worth boyfriend.

CHAPTER FORTY-THREE

THE PRENUPTIAL AGREEMENT –
JUST SAY "NO!"

Sophisticated High Net Worth Men and virtually all divorced high net worth men tend to agree on one thing. Getting married without a prenuptial agreement is the equivalent of economic suicide.

It is possible, even very likely, that your man will insist on a prenuptial agreement as a condition of getting married. Your job is to resist this offensive attempt to limit your economic and legal options by any means necessary.

What is a Prenuptial Agreement?

A prenuptial agreement (affectionately referred to by divorce lawyers as a "pre-nup,") is an agreement with your husband that defines and limits your economic recovery and legal options. It attempts to resolve what will happen when you get divorced, including how much alimony or spousal support you will receive and how your assets and your husband's assets will be divided.

Pre-nups are enforceable in most jurisdictions unless they were entered into under duress or undue influence or without proper legal representation on behalf of the weaker spouse. A pre-nup will allow your husband to cut his losses and get rid of you at a pre agreed cost. If you sign one you will be precluded from litigating for a larger settlement should a divorce occur.

The money you get can be graduated depending on how long the marriage lasts and the agreement may terminate entirely if you stay married for a specified time (e.g., 5, 7 or 10 years). The agreement can also provide that it terminates on your having his child.

High Net Worth Men are generally most concerned about a short unhappy marriage that ends quickly and costs them a great deal of money. As the term of the marriage lengthens they will be more willing to open their wallets.

The Gold Digger who wants to make a big killing and get divorced in a year or less can be stopped cold by a prenuptial agreement. And those of you with a longer investment horizon should be aware that even with the best of intentions your marriage can easily collapse in six months.

Furthermore, a graduated payment scale may actually incentivize him to divorce you before the payment levels kick up by the end of year three. Rumors that Tom Cruise divorced Nicole Kidman largely because their pre-nup was about to expire have been widely discussed.

Use the Pre-nup to Your Advantage

A pre-nup can also contain other agreements and restrictions on your spouse, including living arrangements and even what happens in the event of adultery. The press reported that Jennifer Lopez proposed a draft pre-nup to Ben Affleck which provided for a $5 million fine in the event he committed adultery. Luckily for Ben, that one will never be tested.

The pre-nup can be an opportunity for you to negotiate for important lifestyle elements, including your own car and driver, a personal trainer, periods when you can be on your own several times a week, one yearly vacation apart and a separate residence for you.

He will have to reveal his assets to you as part of the pre-nup process. If he withholds material information, this can void the agreement. One important fact to keep in mind is that child support arrangements cannot be validly agreed in a pre-nup. Once you have children you are going to get custody and large child support payments if you are divorced and there is nothing he can do to prevent this in the pre-nup.

Nevertheless, the pre-nup is an area that is generally fraught with danger for the High-end Gold Digger™. Here are some things you can do about it.

Just Say "No!"

The first line of defense is that you won't agree to a pre-nup under any circumstances. Never ever. Full stop. Period.

This sometimes works if you are forceful enough. Tell him you only plan to marry once, that you would never agree to divorce him anyway and that discussing a pre-nup could irreparably damage your relationship. (It actually could.)

Tell him you believe in marriage for love. Tell him that pre-nups have ruined numerous relationships. Tell him that it is even against your religion.

Taking this position will smoke out how serious he is about insisting on a pre-nup.

Tell Him You Want to Be Married First

Tell him you will think about what happens in a divorce after you get married, not before. This will put him in an awkward position.

Men don't usually have the courage to raise the pre-nup issue until after you are engaged to be married. Many women get very angry when the subject is raised because they feel their man has done a "bait and switch" on them. You can always tell him you would not have accepted his engagement ring had you known he was going to saddle your relationship with a pre-nup. Repeat that you will discuss it after the wedding.

Post-nups can be just as valid as pre-nups. However, your man will likely have little or no leverage to get you to sign a post-nup once you are actually married. At that point you can just say, "No." There is nothing he can do to force you to sign a post-nup after you are married.

When He Won't Take "No" for an Answer

Your mogul may draw a line in the sand. He may tell you, "My way or the highway." You may find that he just isn't going to marry you without a pre-nup. He may have too much at stake to tolerate that kind of risk. Or perhaps his wealthy parents are threatening to disown him unless he gets one.

At this point you have just three choices:

(1) *Walk away.* Whether this makes sense depends on your other options.

(2) *Sign an agreement but negotiate a generous deal, including expiration of the agreement if your marriage lasts five years.* Your deal should include a substantial residence and enough to live on for the rest of your life. You are giving up all your other options to marry. A divorced woman may be regarded as tainted goods by some high net worth men. So if you are going to put your eggs in his basket, tell him you've got to be well compensated for it. To minimize the stress on your relationship, make him hire a good lawyer of your choice to negotiate your side of the deal. Of course, he should pay all of your legal fees. After all the pre-nup was his idea.

(3) *The riskiest course is to say, "Honey, whatever makes you happy. I will sign it but let's just get it over with. I don't even want to read it!"* Taking this approach means you won't have a lawyer and you won't negotiate anything. Just sign the agreement he provides you with. Do so in the presence of a friend of yours if at all possible and make sure you are visibly drunk or sedated. Then write letters to all of your girlfriends, siblings and parents about how your guy "forced" you to sign the agreement. How he "threatened" you if you wouldn't sign and how you never were even given a chance to read it and did not understand it. Then call them up and ask them to save the letters and the post marked envelopes in a secure place. Better yet, ask them to give them to you for safe keeping.

You are laying the groundwork for your future challenge to the pre-nup as an agreement that you were forced to sign under duress and on the grounds that you did not knowingly consent to its provisions.

Many courts will throw out a pre-nup entered into under such circumstances. Once the pre-nup is voided you will be able to sue him to your heart's content. Of course this is a very risky course. A court may well disregard your little charade, particularly if your husband can prove that you read this book.

CHAPTER FORTY-FOUR

DON'T FOOL AROUND WITH THE HELP

Helping the Help Won't Help You

Sleeping with your mogul's chauffer, gardener or butler is bad policy. This holds true both before and after you land your mogul. First, screwing the help is a high risk, low reward activity. If your target catches you kissing his driver or bodyguard he will immediately cross you off his list of potential mates.

You have proven two things by breaking this iron rule: One, you are not trustworthy and two, you are beneath him.

If you are already dating your mogul he will probably dump you instantaneously and may tell all his close friends what happened. This will immediately ruin your reputation and wipe out his whole valuable network of acquaintances as possible future targets. If you have not yet dated him, you never will once he has seen you snog the butler. And forget about plotting with the butler to seduce his boss. The butler's first loyalty will be to his employer, not you. After all, you aren't paying his salary.

We do know one enterprising Gold Digger who dated Billy Joel's driver and then slept with Joel in hopes of leveraging up. This may have poisoned her already slim chances of landing the has-been singer. In any event, Billy recently married a 21-year-old (although the press claims she is 23).

Patty Hearst and Elizabeth Taylor can afford to marry their bodyguards or carpenters. You can't.

There is only one thing to remember about the help.

Don't go there!

Chapter Forty-Five

THE MARRIED MAN

Married men will go to incredible lengths to prevent you from finding out they are married. We know one New York blonde who thought she was engaged to a high net worth real estate mogul (let's call him J.H.). J.H. had given her the big engagement ring and she had moved into his house in Darien, Connecticut. He told her he had been divorced twice before. She started investigating but only found one divorce decree in the court records.

One morning she woke up next to J.H. and he wasn't moving. "He had always told me that if anything ever went wrong, I should call the ex-wife. I did." It turned out that he was still married to the "ex-wife" (who happens to be the daughter of a prominent Manhattan diet doctor). It also turned out that J.H. was dead. Our blonde ended up with nothing but her "engagement" ring. "Fortunately, I hadn't given up my apartment yet," she said.

This little story illustrates an important and easy to remember principle.

Trust no one.

Married men lie about everything. Besides being married, one of the things married men lie about the most is the frequency of sex with their wives. Any married man who is interested in you will swear that he never has sex with his wife.

While it is true that the phenomenon of sex after marriage has become increasingly rare, it cannot be discounted completely. Reports of occasional occurrences, particularly outside of Manhattan, continue to trickle in.

No matter how earnestly he proclaims that he is no longer intimate with his wife and no matter how often he promises to leave her, you must assume he is lying unless he is physically separated and living apart from her.

If they are still living together and you hear reports that his wife has recently gotten a boob job or plastic surgery, you should assume he is still sleeping with her. Reports that they are publicly affectionate are also a bad sign.

Nevertheless, two principal concerns motivate almost all unhappily married men (and almost all married men are unhappily married). First they are desperate for sex. Second they are desperate for time away from their wives. Married men are therefore particularly vulnerable to having an affair with you. But notwithstanding their promises, they are usually not vulnerable to marrying you.

Taking on a married man is like climbing Mt. Everest—a very difficult project. In almost all cases the most you are likely to end up with is some jewelry and a rented apartment in the Trump "Mistress Building" on Manhattan's Central Park South. The chances of him divorcing his wife, sticking with you through the whole grueling process and then marrying you after such a recent disastrous experience with marriage are almost incalculably small.

Savvy Gold Diggers have an iron rule, don't date a man until six months after his official divorce decree has come through. Prior to that he won't be in any mental or emotional state for a serious relationship.

Nevertheless, for the eternal optimist in you, it is true that some relentlessly persistent women have gotten married men away from their wives.

We know of one aggressive young mistress who did manage to get her married man (let's call him B.D.) to divorce his wife and marry her

During the courtship, B.D. took her out almost every night and bought her jewelry and a sable coat. Within one month after B.D. had divorced his wife, he married our girl.

Here's the strange part: he insisted on moving to New Jersey and stopped going out with her in the evenings. No more   lavish trips and no more expensive restaurants. Suprise surprise... It turned out that his business was in trouble and within a year he had lost most of his money. To add insult to injury, B.D. took on another mistress.

There is an apt saying on the High Net Worth Dating Circuit that should be a caution to any woman contemplating a relationship with a married man.

A man who marries his mistress is creating a job vacancy!

PART SIX

High Net Worth Sex

Chapter Forty-Six

HOLDING OUT

Withholding Sex

This is trickier than it seems, and can backfire if not executed with sensitivity. When you stop him as he is rounding third base you can either leave him begging for more or angry and annoyed. Convey how much you like him by your actions. Your words will tell him you need to know him better.

A man does not understand what you are talking about when you tell him you need to know him better. He will sit there racking his brains trying to figure out what it is that you want to know. He doesn't realize you aren't comfortable having sex with him until you figure out whether he fits into your long-term plans. He doesn't understand that you need to feel you are in a relationship with him before you have sex. He has no such concerns. In fact, his only concern is to get your clothes off and his penis inside of you. Deflecting that goal and steering him into relationship building behavior (like taking you out again) until you are comfortable sleeping with him should be your focus. It won't be easy. He may be so persistant that you may have to get up and leave. Make him take you home in a cab if you think you can get rid of him when the cab arrives at your door. Otherwise just make him put you in a cab. And don't forget to ask for the cab fare!

Withholding sex from high net worth men is tricky. They may have a number of other available options. If you don't sleep with him he may call another girl and have her come over that evening. As a rule you will end up sleeping with your target sooner than you intended. There is nothing wrong with this, unless you don't hear from him afterwards. And this just means you misjudged him. When this happens (and it will) chalk it up to experience and don't worry that he hasn't called you.

Don't take it personally. Remember the rule, if he doesn't call, he doesn't exist.

Masturbate Before Your Date

Worried that you will not be able to resist your hunky, rich, eligible guy? Afraid that you are going to lose control and let him prematurely into your La Perla panties?

One solution is to pleasure yourself before you leave the house. This will not only take the edge off your sexual cravings, it will make you more relaxed and less distracted during your date. And you will be far better able to keep things moving without the risk of losing your presence of mind. We recommend masturbating right before you shower. That way you will be clean, fresh and relaxed when you meet your wealthy dinner companion. It also burns a few calories.

What if Your Mogul Doesn't Turn You On?

Have no fear, Vazoplex is here. If your guy has overdosed on Viagra or is just pressing you for sex when you don't want it, this clear, water soluble gel may be the answer. Just place a small amount on your fingertip and apply to the clitoral area. Since it feels to him like your natural moisture, he will never know the difference. Vazoplex makes it easy for you to pretend to enjoy sex with your man.

BJs – The Oral Out

One sure fire way to avoid having sex with your target is to give him a blow job. When you do, make sure it is a mind blowing experience for him. You can ensure this by carefully reading Chapter 48 – "*The High Net Worth Blow Job.*"

CHAPTER FORTY-SEVEN

SEX – THE DO'S AND DON'TS

Having sex with your man will change the dynamics of your dating relationship. Once you have slept with him the balance of power has subtly shifted in his favor. Prior to going to bed with him, he was chasing you, cajoling you, seducing you. You have been leaving him breathless and bothered at the end of every encounter.

Now he's had you. He will think, if I've had her once, I can have her again. Or he may decide to dump you. Some targets may just be targeting you for their Hump & Dump program. Or perhaps they will keep you on edge by not calling you for 72 hours after having sex.

You have given it all up. The ball is now in his court. Whatever he does will determine whether your prior interactions will develop into a lucrative relationship.

One good tip is to make a firm date with him to get together at a specific time and place before you part after the first night.

Another tip is to try to make your first sexual encounter on an evening when you can both spend the entire night together. It is much easier for him to brush you off if you or he leaves immediately after having sex. If either of you have 8:00 a.m. meetings the next morning, think strategically and don't allow him to do it that evening. The stress of having sex for the first time and worrying about being rested for your morning meeting can affect your relationship.

So spend the whole glorious night together, give him the best sex of his life. Then make a plan for your next get together.

CHAPTER FORTY-EIGHT

THE HIGH NET WORTH
BLOW JOB

Chief among the minimum employment skills necessary for success in high net worth dating and marriage are those related to giving an expert blow job. Expertise in this crucial job skill can be the difference between landing your sugar daddy and living on welfare in an undesirable outer borough. It's not for nothing that they call it a "Job."

Learn the Basics

Don't get fancy. A prominent sex columnist told us the four keys to successful oral sex:

1. A firm overhand grip,
2. Constant moisture,
3. A muted gagging reflex and
4. Dogged persistence even in the face of
the most determined soft-off.

Make sure your mouth is moist before you begin. If necessary, have a glass of cool water at hand. Use your tongue, lips and fingers to tingle his balls before you get going. The basic elements are easy to master. Use your thumb and forefinger and middle finger to form a tourniquet around the base of his erection. Take the head in your mouth and slowly draw the entire length of his erection (or as much as you can) into your mouth and down your throat. Begin to slowly bob up and down, moving the shaft in and out of your mouth but keeping the head inside at all times. There is no need for distracting ornamental licking. Don't worry about the firm grip around the base. You have no idea how much pressure a man can take. Now pick up speed. Count to yourself with each bob "1-100, 2-100, 3-100." Move with dizzying speed. You hair should be flying and your breasts bouncing wildly up and down. Make sure the lights are on so he can see your entire erotic performance. Keep this up for five minutes or more. (If you are good, he won't last five minutes!) To speed his coming, squeeze the tourniquet a little tighter.

The Pearl Noose

For added excitement wrap your pearl necklace around the base of the shaft. Squeeze them into the base with your tourniquet. The added pressure will generally achieve highly satisfactory results. Needless to say the pearls should be genuine.

The Hot and Cold Ice Job

Another important and effective technique requires a glass of ice and a mug of hot tea by the bed. Start with a sip of hot tea and then take it from the top. Pause briefly, put an ice cube in your mouth and get back to work. The temperature variations between the ice and the hot tea is usually a big turn on. For added enjoyment, put the tea in one side of your mouth with an ice cube in the other cheek, then mix them together into an iced tea over his erection. For even more fun put Altoids breath mints in either cheek.

To Swallow or Not to Swallow

Letting him climax in your mouth is the most satisfying finish for your man. Keep a doubly firm grip while he is coming so you can control his movement and avoid gagging. Hold it in for a full 30 to 60 seconds after his orgasm–Keep as still as you can! Don't worry. Semen is not fattening. But many women report that it is very filling.

If you won't risk or can't stomach swallowing, there are clever alternatives. As he begins to come keep your strong overhand grip while quickly removing the head from your mouth and rubbing it against the outside of your cheek. Then move your head up and down to create friction on his penis which should now be between your hand and your cheek. As he continues to come, take it in your hand or in your hair. Believe me, he probably won't know the difference. And if you do it properly, he won't care.

CHAPTER FORTY-NINE

THE GOLD DIGGER'S GUIDE TO SEX AND PERVERSIONS

Sex is an Opportunity

Sex is your big chance. If the sex is lousy for him, you won't hear from him again.

You must be uninhibited, passionate and–this is key–do what he wants but is afraid to ask.

Perversions Are a Gold Mine

Many men have dirty secrets. They have fetishes and perversions they don't want to reveal. But they are dying to have you fulfill them. Perversions are not a turn-off. Perversions are an important and potentially rewarding opportunity to give him something other girls won't. Perversions are the way to a man's heart. Here are a few you might run into.

PERVERSIONS

(1) Foot fetishism. (Let him suck your toes for as long as he wants, he'll be sure to buy you something afterwards.)

(2) Your underwear. (Also harmless. Wear what he wants and watch him drool. If he wants to put them on himself let him. And take pictures so you can blackmail him later if he tries to dump you or just for fun.)

(3) Ass licking. (Let him lick away. You can read a book while he does it.)

(4) Infantilism. (Some men like to be kept in diapers. This is good practice for you when you have his real children later.)

(5) Spanking. (Many powerful men have submissive tendencies and like to be spanked, whipped or tied up. These men make perfect husbands. They do what they are told and doing it turns them on. If you meet a man like this thank your lucky stars and marry him. You will rule the roost for the rest of your days.)

(6) Cross dressing. (Another good sign. Anything he does that is embarrassing that you know about is to be encouraged. Go shopping with him to pick out sexy outfits for him to wear. And don't forget to bring the camera.)

(7) Dominant men. (These guys like you to wait on them hand and foot and then tie you up and whip you. This you don't need. The only possibility for a relationship here, is to turn him into your submissive. Many dominant men also have a submissive side. If you can turn him, you can keep him. Otherwise this is no-go territory.)

(8) Homosexuality. (Don't even think about it. Just dump him. You don't want to risk the humiliation of having him leave you for another man. Run the other way now. Of course if he is very rich and willing to pay you extravagantly to be married to him you may wish to consider it.)

(9) Coprophilia. (If he wants you to do number two, it's time to exit. This is dangerous and unsanitary. Of course, if he just wants an occasional Golden Shower, why not? After you let him enjoy your pee, make him take you shopping.)

(10) Enemas. (If you can stomach this and he is into it, he will love you for it. Your move.)

(11) Threesomes. (All heterosexual men want to do it with two girls. The straight man who doesn't has yet to be born. If you have a girlfriend you can trust, do it. The problem is that "a girlfriend you can trust" is a contradiction in terms. The ideal girl is one who is bi-sexual and who is clearly interested in you, not your high net worth boyfriend.)

(12) He likes to eat pussy. (Marry him fast, before one of your girlfriends does!)

(13) Asexuality, impotence or diminished sex drive. (Thank Heavens! with any luck you will never have to do it with him. But beware, some men who claim to suffer from sexual dysfunction are secretly gay.)

There are two things to remember about sex and perversions.

> **First:** Indulge, indulge, indulge!

> **Second:** Take lots of pictures.

When it comes time to put the squeeze on, a picture is worth a thousand words.

The Dilemma – To Swallow or Not to Swallow

To swallow can be risky because you can get HIV. Not swallowing is even more risky, since in his mind it may be grounds for dumping you straightaway.

The solution is to find a sneaky way to get him to take an AIDS test before you do it. The easiest way is to get him to give blood. Tell him this is a cause you believe in. If they take his blood he is not HIV positive. In that case you can safely swallow away. Of course, a more thorough examination is needed to detect genital warts and other venereal diseases. One way to get him to a doctor to check is to claim he has given you something even if it isn't true.

Sex Should Be Safe – Sometimes

Safe sex is the best policy until you have really gotten serious with your guy and after he has had an HIV test. Men who insist on unsafe sex from the beginning are bad risks and should be rejected. As soon as you know he is disease-free, you can start working on your Inadvertent Pregnancy.

Stay on Your Antidepressants

Stay upbeat and stay on your medication. In the summer of 2002, most New York Gold Diggers switched their antidepressants from Zoloft or Prozac to Celexa. Celexa is a good drug but definitely affects a woman's ability to lubricate. Condoms also tend to absorb moisture. To ease your mogul's entry, slip in a little lubricant (Vazoplex, Astroglide or K-Y Jelly) in the bathroom before crawling into bed.

Since Celexa also can affect your ability to come, practice your pretend orgasms. Men don't mind if you fake an orgasm. They know that if you pretend to come, you at least can't nag them about not coming. Remember that marrying a high net worth man is not about your orgasm. It's about what you do for him.

CHAPTER FIFTY

DOMINATING FOR DOLLARS

A significant number of high net worth, high profile men are intensely sexually stimulated by being dominated by a woman. These men may have a wide range of things that stimulate them, from mild spankings to a full on strict bondage lifestyle of torture and humiliation. A somewhat smaller but still significant number of men are dominant themselves. However, the number of submissive men greatly outnumbers the number of women with any interest in indulging these desires.

These men will often drop conversational hints to indicate their interests. Listen carefully for these mentions of leather, latex or spanking in an inappropriate or even a humorous context as these are tipoffs that mean you are dealing with a submissive man.

Submissive Men Can Be Gold Mines

Submissive men like you to tell them what to do. You can often have such men perform all kinds of unreasonable and absurd tasks that will make your life easier. Make him come over and clean your apartment. Make him shine all your shoes. Make him take you shopping. Make him scrub your bathtub or floor. Make him give you a foot or back massage. Make him cook and serve you dinner. All this and more is possible with a man who is sexually turned on by being dominated by a woman.

The more demanding and authoritative you are the more such a man will like you. However, he won't like it if you are indecisive or hesitant about ordering him around. The stricter and more unreasonable you are the better.

The difficulty you will have is transitioning your servant into a husband. You have to make sure he doesn't think of you as someone he meets only to taste forbidden fruit. He has to think of you as a possible life partner, not someone he sees on the side in a compartmentalized relationship.

Keeping It Under Lock and Key

If you really want to make sure he doesn't cheat on you, lock it up and keep the key in your purse.

There are now some very well designed plastic long-term male chastity devices on the market. The CB 2000 (available at the Purple Passion in New York and at many other Sex Shops), even comes with plastic padlocks that your man can wear when he goes through an airport x-ray security system. It consists of a plastic sheet and sheath that surrounds his love bat and a padlock. You keep the key in your purse. It is designed so that it is impossible for your guy to get an erection while he is wearing it. However, it does permit urination and can be worn for weeks at a time.

It is physically impossible for him to have sex or even to climax or get an erection while he is wearing it.

Don't let him leave the house without it!

PART SEVEN

High Net Worth Mating –

The Engagement and Beyond –

(Getting Him on the
Express Train to the Altar)

Chapter Fifty-One

GETTING THE ENGAGEMENT RING YOU DESERVE

You want an engagement ring from Tiffany's. Not just because it costs more, but so that when your girlfriends ask you can say with a toss of your hair,

"Oh. It's from Tiffany's. Isn't it beautiful?"

Of course they will tell you it's beautiful. But they will only really gush if it's big. There is nothing more humiliating than a small engagement ring. Your engagement ring is a symbol of your value and importance as a woman. It's size and design are immediately visible signs of your social status and of your fiancé's place in society.

Don't put up with a small engagement ring!

The Carat and the Stick – Getting the Ring You Deserve

Take your intended to Tiffany's and make him look at the engagement rings. You will need to train him to buy you the right ring.

Tiffany's has a little brochure they give out on the types of engagement rings and the possible types of cuts. Make him read it and show him what you like. Then take him to the counter and ask to see some of the big rings. Ask only to see the ones over three-carats and swoon over the one you like. Tell him it's a ring you couldn't refuse. Get him used to the sticker shock. He should be looking in the $50,000 and up range. If he doesn't blink at that, take him to Harry Winston and really make his eyes pop out.

After that he will be too ashamed to offer you a ring of less than three-carats. You have got to make him understand that he's going to need a big ring to get you. Explain to him a one-carat or less engagement ring screams "insufficient funds" for the entire world to hear.

The good thing about your engagement ring is that you get to keep it even if you get divorced or break off the engagement. (You did a lot of good work to earn it. Why give it back?)

And whether you are divorced or never made it to the altar, your ring can come in handy as a down payment on a condominium on Manhattan's upper East Side.

CHAPTER FIFTY-TWO

YOUR WEDDING IS YOUR BEST REVENGE

It's Party Time!

Your wedding is your victory party. This is no time to hold back. Throw the party of your life and spare no expense. Just make sure hubby agrees to pay for it all. This is not a bill you want to send to your Dad.

While there is a dreadful tradition that the bride's family pays for the wedding this rule goes out the window when your hubby is a high net worth man.

God knows how long you waited for this day, now's the time for your new hubby to pay!

Yes, you do want the Sylvia Weinstock $5,000 wedding cake, the Beluga Caviar, the Chocolate Fountain and the Charles Krug champagne. And why not have it at the Pierre Hotel? Yes, you want everything. While the average American wedding costs just under $25,000, yours should cost $500,000. And why not? Hubby can afford it.

Your wedding is your press announcement to the world that your intended is now taken. He is off the market and he belongs to you. This you need to have highly publicized.

Don't Go Psycho!

The preparations for your wedding can create great stress between you and your future in-laws, your intended, your parents and your girlfriends and ex-boyfriends. You will be assaulted from all sides with demands and requests from family and friends and beset by the constant need to make decisions with your wedding planner, caterer, flower arranger, photographer, cake supplier, bandleader, location manager, dressmaker and loads of other parasites and would be parasites who want something from you. Let's face it, creating your special day of happiness, will be an unmitigated nightmare. The important things are to stay focused, keep cheery and avoid committing homicide whenever possible.

Above all don't go psycho!

There is one main danger in the pre-wedding period which is the risk he might call it off. Beware, just because you are engaged and have set a date and the invitations are printed–don't assume nothing can go wrong.

We know one high net worth nephew of a publishing mogul who called off his wedding to his lovely and ambitious young brunette just one week before the elaborately planned wedding. The couple had to call each guest individually to explain that the bridegroom "just isn't ready for marriage." This kind of public humiliation you don't need.

The time before the wedding is when all his second thoughts will come to the fore. This is when you need to be at your sweetest and sunniest. Don't let him see you screaming at the wedding planner. Your face doesn't look nearly as attractive when it is contorted with rage. If he sees you this way he will wonder when the rage is going to be directed at him.

Men can be amazingly incurious about their own wedding. They usually feel their only job is to put on a tux or a tie and show up. If you have a fiancé like this, praise the Lord and keep him out of all the wedding preparations. Just ask him who he wants to invite (no ex-girlfriends) and where his mother wants to sit at dinner. The morning of the wedding send him off to a spa for a long massage. This way he won't see your last minute hysterics.

The Bridesmaid Dress

This is your chance to shine and, better still, make your girlfriends look bad. Start with a brownish-orange or yellowish-green, ill-cut, calf length bridesmaid dress. Make your bridesmaids wear it with flats that look like bathroom slippers. Tell them they have to purchase it themselves. And make sure it's expensive.

Have lots of pictures taken of your girlfriends in this awful dress and mail them to all your friends after the wedding. That will put your girlfriends in their place.

Your wedding is much more than a spectacular beginning to your life of leisure as a wealthy woman. It is a God-given opportunity to humiliate your girlfriends.

After all, you won't be needing them anymore!

CHAPTER FIFTY-THREE

LIVING WITH A MAN YOU HATE

We Never Promised You a Rose Garden

You may find that you now have everything you ever dreamed of: The houses in Aspen, Palm Beach and Southampton, the snazzy convertible, the Blackglama mink, the enormous diamond ring, the high net worth husband, the Bulgari or Cartier watch, the Hermès alligator Kelly handbag and anything else you feel like charging on your husband's credit card. There is just one problem. You can't stand your man. This happens to most women who marry for love. Imagine how often it happens to women who marry for money.

While your material needs may be taken care of, you may have a man who is:

(1) verbally or physically abusive;

(2) negative or critical of you;

(3) a workaholic you rarely see;

(4) insanely jealous or controlling;

(5) under the thumb of his parents,
    ex-wife or children who despise you;

(6) a womanizer, a gambler, an alcoholic or all three;

(7) fond of strip bars, sports bars and whorehouses;

(8) obsessed with pornography;

(9) a drug addict or alcoholic;

(10) a tightwad;

(11) boring or uncommunicative;

(12) impotent or a lousy lover;

(13) unwilling to let you redecorate;

(14) manipulative and sadistic;

(15) a pathological liar;

(16) depressed or mentally ill;

(17) too short, fat or bald;

(18) uneducated or ill-mannered;

(19) utterly lacking in social skills or any fashion sense;

(20) barely able to speak grammatical English; or

(21) slowly figuring out who you are and liking less and less of what he sees.

Even if your guy has all of these typical high net worth male characteristics, do not despair. Stay positive and cheery. The worse he is, the better off you may end up. Most of the negative characteristics listed above will be worth money in your divorce settlement.

Exploit His Weaknesses

What does a smart Gold Digger do with a guy who has such negative tendencies?

Easy. She keeps records. Detailed records. With tape recordings or even videos of particularly bad behavior. A recording device in your purse or on the phone, a web cam in the bedroom or a concealed video camera that you operate remotely can be a girl's best friends. Take extensive photographs of his pornography collection and sex toys. Encourage him to allow you to videotape any unusual sex activities.

The purpose of the surveillance described above is two-fold, revenge and/or a big divorce settlement.

If he is married to someone else he will not want your recordings to be sent to his wife. If he is married to you he will not want them shown to the judge in your divorce action.

Nor will he want your tapes and transcripts released to the press or sent to his employer or business colleagues. Using your surveillance tapes is not blackmail, it is common sense. Each of your man's negative characteristics whether they involve sex, abusive behavior, drugs or alcohol are all valuable leverage points you can use to negotiate a larger divorce settlement, eliminate rivals or wives or simply get him to generously acknowledge your goodwill in not making them matters of public record.

In the battle of the sexes, weapons are scattered everywhere. You need only think carefully about which ones you want to pick up and use against him.

There is no man without weaknesses. It is up to you to find your man's flaws. A few drinks with one of his ex-girlfriends should tell you where to look. If you can afford it, having him followed by a private investigator can also be useful. Often a man's weaknesses are fairly obvious. In some cases, he may even tell you about them, particularly weaknesses of the sexual variety. In other cases he will be too embarrassed to admit them.

Search His Apartment Thoroughly

The first time he leaves you alone in his apartment, search it. We don't mean look in the bathroom cabinet and rifle through his drawers. We mean look everywhere and through everything, leave no closet or drawer unexamined. Leave no shoebox unopened. Look through his old correspondence. Examine his telephone address books, printouts and palm pilots. Get into his computer and read his e-mail and look at his favorite sites to check his real interests. Run your hands along the inside of each drawer and underneath his clothes. Look behind the books on the bookshelf. Anything you find (or don't find) is information.

Any good divorce lawyer will tell you that you can extract a larger divorce settlement if your high net worth husband has been abusive or violent, cheated on you repeatedly or is addicted to drugs or alcohol.

Remember: The secrets you don't discover now can cost you money later. Get the truth and you can get a big divorce settlement.

Once your divorce settlement comes through, you will be able to start your husband hunting all over again.

The Jack Rabbit

There is one essential tool for surviving life with a husband you hate. Your vibrator.

We recommend The Jack Rabbit. The Rabbit is economical and effective. It has parts that circle, "ears" that come out of the top and it runs so smoothly you can use it while lying in bed next to your sleeping husband. *Toys in Babeland* has the best selection of women's sex toys, including machines even more advanced than the Rabbit. The store on Mercer Street in New York's SoHo area is great fun to visit and the staff is knowledgeable and female oriented.

Buy it before the wedding. You may find you need it before you get back from the honeymoon!

Remember: The great thing about Gold Digging is that getting there is half the fun!

Happy Gold Digging!

CHAPTER FIFTY-FOUR

THE GOLD DIGGER'S ALPHABET™

"A" is for Anorexic and that we are not.

"B" is for Bulimia and that we don't fear.

"C" is for the Cash that we feel coming near.

"D" is for the happy Dance we do when hubby passes on.

"E" is for the big Engagement ring we will soon have.

"F" is for the Food we do not eat.

"G" is for all the Gold that will soon be ours.

"H" is for Hubby, that sweet rich old guy.

"I" is for how Itsy-bitsy we are.

"J" is for the Jaguar hubby got for our birthday.

"K" is for the Kitchen – we're not sure where it is.

"L" is for the Life of Leisure we will soon lead.

"M" is for the Men we ensnare in our honeyed trap.

"N" is for the Nightmare of losing those last extra pounds.

"O" is for the Oval our botoxed lips make.

"P" is for the Pain we suffer to be beautiful.

"Q" is for how Quickly we will be married and rich.

"R" is for the Riches our Gold Digging will bring us.

"S" is for all the Shoes hubby will be buying us.

"T" is for our Titties, those weapons of war.

"U" is for our Underwear from La Perla, Wolford and Agent Provocateur.

"V" is for that special place that wealth worships most.

"W" is for all the Work we will never have to do.

"X" marks the spot where we sign our marriage license.

"Y" is for the *Yenta* we certainly are.

"Z" is for the ZZZ's we catch as we snooze by the pool.

So please wish us luck, we are thin, rich and well,
We don't eat much but we look better than Hell!

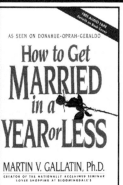

HOW TO GET MARRIED IN A YEAR OR LESS
by Dr. M. Gallatin

Have we got a book for you! These strategies are literally guaranteed to work–or your money back!
The author was featured on *Oprah* and in *The NY Times*. These well thought out tips, tactics & techniques also tell you where to go to meet the right people, and how to act when you do! A great gift for both men and women, young and old!

Retail Price: $17.95 • Special Price: $14.95

Cloth • 6" x 9" • 276 pgs • Illustrations • ISBN: 1-56171-980-3

MEN WHO HATE THEMSELVES– AND THE WOMEN WHO AGREE WITH THEM
by Davis Rudnitsky, M.D.

If you're looking for a great relationship, don't buy this book! If you're looking for lots of deep and meaningful insights that will finally bring you the intimacy and love you deserve... forget about it!
But if you want to laugh all the way to your shock treatments, then this is the book for you.

Retail Price: $4.99 • Special Price: $3.99

Soft • 4" x 7" • 192 pgs • ISBN: 1-56171-276-0

I WORSHIP THE VERY DIRT SHE TREATS ME LIKE: *The Story Of a Warm & Caring Guy In a Society Of Cold And Calculating Women*
by Josh Raphaelson and Jay Silverstein

The perfect book to leave on your coffee table–if you want your guests to howl with laughter.
The cover alone is priceless. Featured on *Salley Jesse Rafael*, *CNN*, and *Oprah*.

Retail Price: $4.99 • Special Price: $3.99

Soft • 4" x 7" • 200 pgs • Illustrations

THE JOY OF DEPPRESSION
by David Rudnitsky, M.D.

A hilarious comic send-up of all the popular self-help guides. The author is a noted neurotic, who humorously covers every aspect of being depressed.

Packed with outrageous illustrations.

Retail Price: $4.99 • Special Price: $3.99

Soft • 4" x 7" • 192 pgs • Illus. • ISBN: 1-56171-273-6

IS HE FOR REAL?: *Knowing Sooner What A Man Will Be Like Later*
by David Samson & Elayne J. Kahn, Ph.D.

This powerful guide, pached with intimate details, finally gives women the upper hand in deciding who's Mr Right–and definitely who's Mr. Wrong! Written by a comedian and a Harvard Ph.D., the authors get to the heart of understanding men's "Secret Signals Of Romance". Read this book and you are guaranteed to learn how to decipher all of his hidden Love Codes!

Retail Price: $12.95 • Special Price: $10.95

Hard • 6" x 6" • 160 pgs • ISBN: 1-56171-985-4

THE MARILYN FILES
by Robert Slatzer

This definitive story of Marilyn's murder will shock you. Contains personal details from Monroe's ex-husbend, author Bob Slatzer, who maintained a close relationship throughout her life. Provides an exhaustive and well-researched analysis of all the circumstances surrounding Marilyn's death. Reveals a wide variety of scenarios, identifies all the possible suspects including RFK and even JFK. With expert testimony to back it up, the book calls for a reopening of the murder case.

Retail Price: $5.99 • Special Price: $4.99

Soft • 4" x 7" • 314 pgs • ISBN: 1-56171-147-0

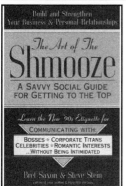

THE ART OF THE SHMOOZE:
A Savvy Social Guide for Getting to the Top • by Bret Saxon & Steve Stein

From the bestselling authors of the definitive book on meeting celebrities (How To Meet & Hang Out With the Stars) comes this ambitious, sophisticated guide to approaching and establishing rapport with anyone in a superior position. The fawning deference and awe that we were always taught to show higher-ups only boomerangs in one's face today. This is the ultimate book for business networking.

Retail Price: $21.95 • Special Price: $14.95

Paper • 4.5" x 7.5" • 304 pgs • Photos • ISBN: 1-56171-175-6

HELP YOURSELF TO HAPPINESS: *See Yourself In A Whole New Way*
by Gerald Jackson

What's holding you back? If you are one of the very few who has mastered the art of living, then put down this book! However, if you are still looking for the secrets of happiness, health, and prosperous living, then read on, because this book was written for you!

Retail Price: $5.50 • Special Price: $4.99

Cloth • 4" x 7" • 260 pgs • ISBN: 1-56171-314-4

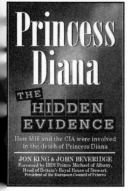

PRINCESS DIANA: *The Hidden Evidence*
by Jon King & John Beveridge

Was Princess Diana murdered? Or was she the victim of an innocent though tragic accident? If she was murdered, who did it? Who ordered the killing and what were their motives.

Based on information received from a veteran CIA contract agent one week prior to the crash in Paris–plus further evidence obtained from other highly placed sources, this investigative work presents an uncompromising inquiry into Diana's death.

This thoroughly researched book reveals the shocking truth behind the most scandalous, closely guarded secret in the UK's history.

Retail Price: $24.95 • Special Price: $19.95

Hard • 6" x 9" • 432 pgs • ISBN: 1-56171-922-6

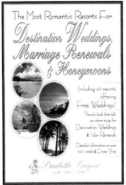